To Ken

Re-presenting the Metropolis

Architecture, urban experience and social life in London 1800–1840

Dana Arnold

ASHGATE

The author has asserted her right under the Copyright, Designs and Patents Act, 1988, to be identified as the author of this work.

Published by
Ashgate Publishing Limited
Gower House
Croft Road
Aldershot
Hants GU11 3HR
England

Ashgate Publishing Company
131 Main Street
Burlington
Vermont 05401-5600
USA

Ashgate website: http://www.ashgate.com

British Library Cataloguing-in-Publication data

Arnold, Dana
  Re-presenting the metropolis: architecture, urban
experience and social life in London 1800–1840
  1. City planning – England – London – History – 19th century
  2. Urban landscape architecture – Social aspects – England –
London – History – 19th century 3. City and town life –
England – London – History – 19th century 4. Architecture –
England – London – History – 19th century 5. London
(England) – History – 19th century
  I.Title
  711.4'09421'09034

Library of Congress Cataloging-in-Publication data
  Re-presenting the metropolis: architecture, urban experience and social life in
London, 1800–1840 / Dana Arnold
    p. cm.
  Includes bibliographical references.
    1. London (England) – Social life and customs – 19th century. 2. City and town
life – England – London – History – 19th century. 3. City planning – England –
London – History – 19th century. 4. Architecture – England – London – History –
19th century. I.Title.

DA683 .A76 2000
711.4'0942109034–dc21

ISBN 1 84014 232 4

Printed on acid-free paper

00–030575

Typeset in Palatino by Manton Typesetters, Louth, Lincolnshire, UK and printed in Great Britain by The University Press, Cambridge.

Contents

Abbreviations

Cres   Crown Estate Papers

HKW   J.M. Crook and M.H. Port, *The History of the King's Works*, Vol VI, London, HMSO, 1970

PRO   Public Records Office

Figures

Acknowledgements

The research for this book was carried out over several years and I would like to thank the staff of the many archives I used for their help in locating material. These include the Guildhall Library, the Museum of London, Sir John Soane's Museum, the Paul Mellon Centre for Studies in British Art, the Public Record Office, the Victoria and Albert Museum and the Yale Center for British Art. I must also thank Professor Andrew Ballantyne and Professor Adrian Rifkin who kindly read and commented on the final draft; any omissions are my own.

I am also indebted to Abigail Moore for compiling the index and to Dr Lucy Peltz and Sarah Sears without whom the collation of such a wide range of visual material would not have been possible. My editor Pamela Edwardes has been a model of patience and encouragement and Ellen Keeling has been most helpful during the production of this book for which I am most appreciative. Finally, I should like to thank my husband Dr Ken Haynes for his support and forbearance while I was writing the text.

Introduction

This book re-presents the metropolis by mapping key developments in London's architecture and planning, 1800–1840, against the social and cultural framework of the city. One of the principal lines of enquiry is the evolution of an urban self-consciousness and its influence on the development and experience of London, particularly from the point of view of the urban bourgeoisie. The awareness of the city as a complete and living entity did much to shape social life and posits the notion of the city as a consciously constructed artefact. As such, emotional responses to its form and content are possible and these play a fundamental role in the shaping of urban experience. The city can then be presented as an emblematic expression of different kinds of identities relating to gender, class and nationhood.

The chapters in this volume concentrate on developments in urban planning, infrastructure and architecture in London in the first decades of the nineteenth century. The principal areas of interest are the creation of public open spaces, new roads and bridges, national monuments and buildings for show including museums, galleries and private townhouses. Evidence of attitudes towards the metropolis is drawn from a range of written sources including contemporary commentators, guidebooks, Parliamentary Reports and Enquiries, and literary references to the city. This study challenges the canon of presenting urban environments within the biographical frameworks of architects and patrons or as the result of socio-economic and political forces. The quality of urban experience formed by sensory responses to the city allows the exploration of the dynamic between city and society which has resonance for the broader cultural understanding of urban form. This sets up a new paradigm for the study of metropolitan history with London as a matrix of key architectural, social and cultural issues.

The thematic exploration of London covers at once its perimeters and approaches as defining mechanisms of the metropolis; the re-orientation of its streets and axes and their impact on urban experience through modes of travel and circulation. Alongside this the city as an expression of different kinds of authority and as a site and sight of spectacle and display formulate a notion of social life. Here the urban bourgeoisie – a middle class in the making – who stand distinct from their eighteenth-century predecessors through their numbers and their vital role in the metropolitan governmental systems and economy are the main focus of study. The urban experience of this social group, identified here by the interchangeable use of the terms bourgeois and middle class, has remained uncharted and this book attempts to map its emergence as a potent political and economic force through the interaction and differences between a range of sociological and cultural historical perspectives on London. The London bourgeoisie were flâneurs/euses – Baudelaire's strolling observers of the 'landscapes of the great cities' who felt at home in the anonymous flow of the urban crowd. The sensitivity of the flâneurs/euses to the signs and impressions of the 'outward show of life' gave them the analytical sophistication to reveal the meanings of the city, which makes them ideal interlocutors between important moments in London's histories and the present day. The flâneur/euse was part of Baudelaire's project to capture the ephemeral and contingent newness of the present which constituted the idea of modernity. Baudelaire's assertion that the encountering of newness is disturbing and that this fundamental aspect of modern life is manifest in the representational spaces of the metropolis suggests that the urban experience of social life of the bourgeoisie provides a more compelling narrative of modernity than a survey of grand projects and chronological change. This focus on the middle class allows an investigation into the experience of this significant group at a time of change and on the eve of a period of even greater social and political upheaval. As such it is a contrasting preamble to the rich and widely discussed documentation on the condition of the working classes in the middle years of the nineteenth century by authors such as Marx, Engels and Mayhew.

The chapters of this book cover the expansion of London – that is the City of London on its eastern side, the City of Westminster on its west and the Borough of Southwark on the south bank of the Thames – in terms of geographical size and population. The spread west as fashionable society vacated the City for the modern squares of the West End had an impact on London's boundaries which were pushed further outwards. This growth and re-orientation of London changed the city's relationship with the river Thames and redefined its entrance points. These changes had consequences for the urban infrastructure of London which changed from insular garden squares and pockets of tangled medieval street plans to an integrated whole. New axes, including the New Street, later Regent Street, (1812–21) running north–south linking the Regent's Park with Charing Cross and the New

Road, later Marylebone Road, running east–west across the northern edge of London, were established whilst The Mall and Piccadilly assumed greater importance in the city plan. These axes altered the experience of the metropolis by making London a more cohesive entity through their connections with entrance ways and their re-orientation of circulation and vista. The latter was important as it focused attention on selected places or buildings, most notably Trafalgar Square, Carlton House (demolished in 1827) and Buckingham Palace.

Ways of circulating through and travel times across London became increasingly important issues in the opening years of the nineteenth century and impacted on the nature of urban experience. Regent Street forged an important link between residential and commercial areas and royal processional routes through London added a political dimension to circulatory patterns. Alongside this, public walks and rides became an increasingly effective way of influencing how the city was encountered and this issue became the subject of Parliamentary Reports on the Royal Parks and a Commission on Public Walks. The hegemonic role of representations of authority was a hallmark of urban experience and was manifest not only in the creation of new vistas and circulatory patterns but also in new buildings and the changing significance of place. New barracks, palaces and governmental offices punctuated the cityscape as symbols of authority through their architecture and function, whilst Charing Cross and Hyde Park Corner offered different kinds of urban experience enhanced by the strategic placing of monuments to the monarchy and the nation.

The celebration of both the city and the nation became a social activity in this new modern metropolis. The dioramas and panoramas of London, like the one in the Colosseum (1827) in the Regent's Park, made the city a delight for the senses. Interaction between those in a specific social group was encouraged not only in the Royal Parks but also in the proliferation of public and private museums, galleries, places of entertainment and institutions. The new wealthy middle class, which lacked the comfort of lineage, expressed itself through professional and academic institutions and clubs. The array of smart new clubhouses on Pall Mall, with their distinguished membership lists, replaced the Court as a nexus for polite society and helped to define a social identity for the bourgeoisie. The architecture of the Athenaeum (1827) or the Reform Club (1838) employed the iconography of past civilisations to enhance this emerging, male-dominated middle class. Public collections such as the British Museum (1823) and the National Gallery (1827) provided venues for social intercourse and the appreciation of the political and cultural significance of the objects on display, which in turn gave a sense of empowerment through knowledge. And the importance of display to social life in London also manifested itself both in private collections held in the townhouses and in the shopping arcades and manufacturers' showrooms which fed the ever-growing appetite for consumer goods.

These different systems for re-presenting London are not necessarily counterpoints but rather they form a complex set of social, economic and cultural relationships. London's infrastructure, architecture and geography remained in a state of flux in the period *c*. 1800–1840. And this vast totality of the metropolis has to be brought to scale so that it may be interpreted and understood. In this way each chapter provides a thematic walk around a different aspect of London which runs parallel to and intersects with the book as a whole. Just as objects and commodities take on a system of meanings relating to the religious, aesthetic and social values relevant to their time, so do cities. But in this case these meanings are not static as cities continually change and develop over time without entirely shedding their past. Historical sequences cannot then be expressed in spatial terms; space, or indeed a city, cannot have two different simultaneous contents, instead histories of the same geographical location must be juxtaposed. In this way the thematic representations of London, whether relating to the real, the virtual or the subconscious are not at variance, rather they reinforce the city's diversity. These different explorations of London confront the traditional chronological narratives of the city and instead signify moments in the city's histories whilst remaining fragments of a whole. These discontinuities result in the presentation and re-presentation of architecture and events that shaped urban experience and social life in London in the opening decades of the nineteenth century. Consequently buildings, planning projects and events appear in the chapters at different moments of their evolution and histories as they are multi-faceted parts of the intertwined narratives of London.

This book surveys the varied nature of contemporary evidence both written and visual. The selection of contemporary sources is important as they are set within a range of paradigms from social and cultural theory as a means of exploring the perceptions and practices of everyday life in the early nineteenth-century metropolis. The divisions between these areas are not always clearly defined and the resonance between sources and themes is part of the intellectual project of this book, which leads to the question 'What are the constituent parts of the culture and society of London at a given moment in time?' In answer to this it can be stated that the feel of the city in terms of the psychological responses to the new urban environment and the physical reality of the crowds and the constant movement and state of flux can cohere at certain times in the anonymous, isolated flâneur and the institutional and social interactions that exist within a metropolitan framework. The weaving in of new technologies to the metropolitan infrastructure of transport, lighting and police are important as they present the city as a machine with a kind of ambivalent modernity. The underlying question of modernity and how the city can be used as a metaphor for this underpins much of the discussion in this book. New social relations and metropolitan circumstances in the opening years of the nineteenth century redefined the city and presented an urban environment that embraced the present with all its innovations and reconfigured the past to represent its make-up and aspirations. The way in which a city can function and evolve as a means of expressing urban experience and social life can reveal modern ways of seeing. These themes reveal the complex set of relationships and interconnected symbolic, economic and administrative facets of London. But each of these elements has to be read as it is inferred in the totality of the metropolis and is not immediately apparent in more linear chronological surveys.

The city is not then just a set of buildings in a specific geographical location – the dialectic between architecture and the city and their interrelation is an indicator of metropolitan identity which is an agglomeration of histories, geographies, social relationships, production, consumption and governmental institutions. In this way the city becomes a representation of an imagined community or environment which encompasses the symbol or metaphor and the discourses through which notions of modernity and urban experience can be expressed and explored. A city like any building or work of art is text that can be read and is open to multiple and varied interpretations which can explore the resonance between different discourses relevant to social and cultural theory. These theoretical paradigms are used to re-present the metropolis and to improve its legibility with specific regard to its architecture, urban experience and social life.

This volume is intended to complement the existing body of writing on London whilst embracing studies and approaches to the historical narratives of other cities. The combination of the aesthetic with the psychological, the social with the political, as seen in Georg Simmel's classic essay *The Metropolis and Mental Life*, and the writings of Charles Baudelaire and Walter Benjamin about Parisian life in the nineteenth century are a starting point for this intellectual project. Paris remains a foil for London and Richard Sennett's *The Fall of Public Man* (1974) is an exemplary sociological study of the French capital in the nineteenth century. The theoretical paradigms for the approach and method of this book are those set up by Michel Foucault in *The Order of Things: an archaeology of human sciences* (1970) and *The Archaeology of Knowledge* (1972). Foucault's ideas about the heterotopic and heterochronic functions of space as expressed in *Of Other Spaces* (*Des Espaces Autres*), where a city or the elements that constitute it can become a counter-site which re-enacts, represents and inverts the utopian mirror image of the metropolis, relate specifically to the fragmentation and re-representation of London in all its complexities. And Foucault's theory of the panopticon and its relationship to ways of seeing and the complexity of governmental power structures, as developed in *The Order of Things: an archaeology of human sciences*, and *Discipline and Punish: the birth of the prison* (1979), informs the discussion of how the city was viewed and the relationship of the individual to the whole. These theoretical models combine and interact to enable us to see London in its space–time location through a kaleidoscopic image of spatial oppositions, social rituals and cultural practices.

London has become a popular subject of study in recent years and has been approached in a variety of ways and it is hoped that this study will enrich this body of work. The rich visual and literary sources for London's histories can be found in the exhibition catalogue *London – World City 1800–1840* (Fox 1992) and in Rick Allen's literary anthology *The Moving Pageant: a literary source book on London street-life, 1700–1914* (1998). The literary image of London is also the concern of Julian Wolfreys *Writing London* (1998) which focuses on the nineteenth century. Visual records of the city from this time are discussed in Alex Pott's article 'Picturing the Modern Metropolis' *History Workshop Journal* (1988) and Griselda Pollock's analysis of late nineteenth-century images of London in 'Vicarious Excitements; London; A pilgrimage by Gustave Doré and Blanchard Jerrold', *New Formations* (1988). The issues surrounding the different identities of London at key moments in its histories are the subject of the essays in my edited volume *The Metropolis and its Image: constructing identities for London* (1999). In many of these writings St Paul's emerges as a touchstone of London's identity and a symbol of the city, and Stephen Daniels's opening chapter of *Fields of Vision* (1986) 'The Prince of Wales and the Shadow of St Paul's' discusses the relationship between the Cathedral and the metropolis. This juxtaposition of space and history coheres in the loaded symbolic presence of St Paul's and it is here that this study begins.

Dana Arnold

The View from St Paul's

St Paul's Cathedral stands as a symbol of the metropolis and of the nation and by virtue of its dome[1] as an *axis mundi* linking London and the country with the rest of the Empire. It is a signifier of the urban renewal of London after the Great Fire of 1666. The combination of church and state, national and local government necessary to enable this rebuilding programme marked the beginning of the rise of national and civic systems of authority. But more than this St Paul's remains the viewing platform for London. From atop its dome it is possible to survey the metropolis and to appreciate the intricacies of the streetplan, the course of the river and, on a clear day, to get a sense of the shape, both metaphorical and physical, of the city.

The fascination with the view from St Paul's pervaded the experience of London in 1800–1840 for visitors, temporary residents and real Londoners or 'cockneys' alike. St Paul's remains the starting point both for viewing the city from within its physical perimeter and for discourses around the metaphorical and psychological experiences of the metropolis. This view, according to the journalist Robert Mudie, formed 'a panorama of industry and of life more astonishing than could be gazed upon from any other point'.[2] The writer sees the metropolis as a modern Babylon, resplendent, opulent yet morally degenerate. The great building projects of the West End and the spread of the city across to the south bank of the Thames signalled national and metropolitan greatness in the same way as the rebuilding of St Paul's had done after the Great Fire of 1666. This reinforced the primacy of the metropolis and its central position in the conceptual map of the British Isles and the Empire.

Even when the size and shape of the city had expanded westwards to leave the Cathedral in its dislocated position in the City the view from its cupola remained central to the way London was conceived of and seen as a complete entity. The heart of the metropolis was now focused around West-

1.1   Decimus Burton, The Colosseum, Regent's Park, 1823–7

minster and Charing Cross and with the development of the Regent's Park
was expanding northwards on a new axis. The Colosseum (1823–7) stood on
this new central north–south median on the eastern edge of the Regent's
Park (Figure 1.1).[3] The building housed a panoramic perspectival view of
London painted by E. T. Parris based on drawings by the proprietor Thomas
Hornor which he had made from the actual vantage point of the cupola of St
Paul's Cathedral (Figure 1.2). Visitors ascended to a viewing platform in the
centre of the building via the first hydraulic lift, which was designed specially for this purpose. From there the whole of London could be seen, as if
from the top of St Paul's, including the Colosseum itself. The *Mechanics'
Magazine* gave a detailed account of the experience before its final completion in 1829:

Quite enough is already apparent, to justify the belief that the view will be at once
the most striking and curious that has ever yet been exhibited. ... The effect is
exactly similar to that produced by looking from the top of St Paul's, with this
difference – that in the Coliseum you may command a constantly clear atmosphere,
and are spared the labour of mounting the never ending stairs which the enterpris-
ing cockneys, who condemn themselves to ascend the heights of the metropolitan
church, are obliged to tread.[4]

1.2   Bird's eye view from the Pavilion in the Colosseum, Regent's Park

The lack of the physical exertion of ascending to the top of St Paul's on the part of the viewer in no way compromised the experience or the 'realism' of the view from the Cathedral. The account continued

The drawing is executed with such a degree of precision … the most exact geometrical results have been obtained throughout the picture, and to such an extent has this accuracy been carried, that the most minute objects to which the range of the view extends may be discerned by the naked eye, and satisfactorily identified by means of glasses. The painting … keep[s] up the illusive idea of distance in a manner which is perfectly astonishing … the spectator finds it difficult … to believe that his eyes are fixed on a plain surface.[5]

Hornor complemented the Colosseum with the publication of a book of engravings based on his panorama.[6] This offered a different experience from the Colosseum panorama of the city as a macrocosm, and the text prompted a celebration and appreciation of its shape and form and the differences between London and other major European cities including Paris and Rome, which provided a benchmark for the processes of metropolitan development and renewal. Hornor also focused on the characteristics of specific areas, encouraging a comparison between them and between the major public buildings spread across London. The proliferation of visual and textual surveys and guides to London in the opening years of the nineteenth century meant that the metropolis was available to a broad range of publics through a variety of formats. In this way Hornor's re-presentation of the city was part of the new visual culture which commodified the viewer's encounter with the metropolis. And the specific nature of the representation of London in volumes such as Hornor's reconfigured and shaped the nature of memory and urban experience.

Panoptic visions

The role of sight in the experience of the metropolis had a special significance in the opening years of the nineteenth century. This centres on two main themes: the social relations of looking or what might now be called the flâneur/euse and the Foucauldian idea of 'un régime panoptique'.[7] Both these concepts are closely related to the notion of modernity which was fundamental to the architecture, urban experience and social life of London at this time. The visual register of the city was at once static – the panoptic vision – and fluid – the mobile and subjective gaze of the flâneur/euse. The latter implies a gendered experience of the city but the early nineteenth-century metropolis resisted this division. The relationship between male and female usually centres on the feminine being the subject of the masculine gaze. But within this metropolitan context the relationship of flâneur to flâneuse was not always one of viewer and viewed.[8] Instead the city itself became the object of scrutiny. The panorama offered by the Colosseum extended the field of the visible in terms of the experience of the metropolis and offered a re-ordering of the power and knowledge of the viewer. Jeremy Bentham's *Panopticon* (1791) consolidated the late eighteenth-century pre-occupation with optical research and theories of seeing which were the product of enlightenment thinking. The panopticon device was a polygonal structure with a central viewing tower for the whole of the interior. The basic design of the building was a 'seeing machine' for use as a prison, factory, hospital or asylum. The experiential world was confined within the panopticon where the *surveillance* or the discipline of the observer was imposed on the observed.[9] Foucault described how Bentham's notion of a static scopic regime as a power system could be translated into broader social structures:

The seeing machine was once a sort of dark room into which individuals spied; it has become a transparent building in which the exercise of power may be super-vised by society as a whole.[10]

Visions of the city, the world or historical events were popular features of the early nineteenth-century metropolis. Wordsworth remarked that

> And, next to these, those mimetic sights that ape
> The absolute presence of reality
> Expressing as in mirror sea and land,
> ...
> Whether the painter – fashioning a work
> To Nature's circumambient scenery
> (*The Prelude*, vii. 248–50 and 256–7)

Panoramas became a kind of Grand Tour for the bourgeoisie[11] and the feeling of expanded knowledge through the representations of the past and present were a form of cultural empowerment. This bourgeois metropolitan hegemony was heightened by the commodification of architecture, history and the city itself as a consumable spectacle. The panorama provided by the Colosseum gave the illusion of spatial and temporal mobility to produce 'the absolute presence of reality'. The viewer appeared to move through the city but in fact remained static. There is a paradox here between the direct fluid experience of the streets of the flâneur/euse and the illusion of London through the virtual gaze of the panorama. Viewing from the platform of the Colosseum was a collective experience which released the spectator from the constraints of the everyday. The passive reception of this re-presentation of London empowered the viewer with a feeling of mastery over the constraints of space and time and fulfilled the social desire for understanding and control.

Invisible panoramas

The metropolis was experienced through senses other than sight.[12] And the dome of St Paul's is also the starting point for the metaphorical and moralistic panorama of London. Early in the century Robert Southey recognised the sublime qualities of the capital which filled 'the imagination to the utmost of its powers'.[13] Charles Dickens uses the vantage point of St Paul's to present his commentary on London life which avoids a physical description of the city in *Master Humphrey's Clock* (1841). Here the added dimension of the city as an organic, living being with a 'mighty heart' posits the notion of the metropolis having an independent life force which helps to shape urban experience. The Cathedral is presented as being so central to the life force of the city that the ticking of its clock set into one of the towers on the west front is the heartbeat of the metropolis.

Images of London as the physical personification and embodiment of the nation pervade writings on the metropolis in the early nineteenth century. Just as St Paul's carried the word *Resurgam* as a symbol of the city's rebuilding after the Great Fire so the developments in the city and the Metropolitan Improvements represent a further layering of new on old and a process of encroachment on the fields and open land scattered across the city, particularly to the west. In Lambert's *History and Survey of London* (1806) the significance of London for the country is recognised as the author states in his advertisement for the guidebook that he attempts 'to satisfy the imaginative minds which must be all over given the extent of the influence of the metropolis on the country'.[14] London played an important part in the national imagination. Its form and meaning were presented to the populace through literature, guidebooks and visual images. These representations of London appealed to a variety of senses and St Paul's remained a fundamental element in all these media.

From the outside looking in

The view and experience of the metropolis from the exterior was very different. The panopticon-like scopic regime from the inside afforded a view of the perimeter of the city. From the outside London has no such definable shape and the view from the suburbs is perhaps then a conceptual one. This is ably expressed by Prince Pückler-Muskau who visited London in the mid-1820s. His thoughts on the view from the outskirts of the city has resonance with Mudie's idea of London as Babylon or Babel:

In an hour's riding I reached a hill ... The sun darted its rays ... like a huge torch ... the centre of which rested directly on the metropolis of this world, – the immeasurable

Babel which lay outstretched with its thousand towers, and its hundred thousand sins, its fog and smoke, its treasures and misery, further than the eye could reach.[15]

The notion of London as Babel is also found in Byron's *Don Juan* where he describes his hero's approach to London:

> Through this, and much, and more, is the approach
> Of travellers to mighty Babylon:
> Whether they come by horse, or chaise, or coach,
> With slight exceptions, all the ways seem one.
> (*Don Juan*, XI. xxiii)

From the outside the perimeter of the city is pierced only by the arterial roads which connected the capital to the rest of the country. These 'macadamized sloughs'[16] terminated in London and underline the city's importance to the country as a whole. These included the principal route from the north, which ran through Islington into the City; the Great West Road, which connected Bath with Piccadilly and the West End; and the King's Road, which linked Richmond Park and the south west with St James's. Thomas de Quincey in his *The Nation of London* (1834) presents London rather like a new Rome to where all roads lead. It is a magnet to which the rest of the country is drawn. De Quincey's description of the volume of cattle being driven to London for sale and slaughter gives a potent image of the city as an irresistible force expressed, once again, in anthropological terms:

I have felt a sublime expression of her [London's] magnitude ... [the cattle] all with their heads pointed to London, and expounding the size of the attracting body, together with the force of its attracting power ... A suction so powerful, felt along radii so vast, and a consciousness, at the same time, that upon other radii still more vast, both by land and by sea, the same suction is operating.

The volume of traffic on the main turnpike roads and their importance to the national infrastructure is highlighted by Byron who describes Juan's journey

> Through coaches, drays, choked turnpikes, and a whirl
> Of wheels, and roar of voices and confusion;
> Here taverns wooing to a pint of 'purl',
> There mails fast flying off like a delusion
> (*Don Juan*, XI. xxii)

Despite its magnetic pull and status as the nexus of the national road system London had a buffer zone around it which gave it a defined shape. This was described in *The Ambulator* in 1811 as being about seven miles long and between two to four miles deep. London, according to this and most other guides comprised only the cities of London and Westminster and the Borough of Southwark on the south bank of the Thames. From the late eighteenth century onwards London was seen as having a ring of villas around it providing in the words of William Cowper:

>The villas with which London stands begirt
>like a swarth Indian with his belt of beads
>('The Task', 1785)

By the second decade of the century the size and shape of London had grown considerably to encompass many of the villas, and this spread was remarked upon in Percy's *History* as continuing and 'swallowing up every villa in its [London's] environs and making them part of the great capital'.[17] Even the former suburban villages of Islington and Hackney were now encompassed by the expanding metropolis.

But there were still suburbs – albeit at a considerable distance as noted by Prince Pückler-Muskau: 'my ride this morning brought me about thirty miles from town. In variety and richness the suburbs of London surpass those of any other capital.'[18] The suburbs had a life of their own which related to but was distinct from the metropolis and they were included in many guides to London in such terms.[19] This is recognised in *The Ambulator* in 1811 where the suburbs are given a separate section. Their difference is recognised further by Lambert who remarked that they have no common government and so should be treated as separate villages.[20]

London's people

The city did not then just gradually dissipate: it was a defined entity. But the prodigious growth of the metropolis in both physical size and population in the opening years of the nineteenth century changed the balance of London in terms of its infrastructure and demography. The population which included the residents of the cities of London and Westminster and the Borough of Southwark had not significantly increased in the first 50 years of the eighteenth century, remaining at around 675,000.[21] But by the first census in 1801 the population of London had reached 864,845. By 1811 this had grown to 1,099,104. In the next 10 years it increased by nearly 20 per cent to 1,225,965 and had reached just under two million by 1841. But up until the end of the seventeenth century the capital was mostly made up of the City of London in terms of its size and population. Moreover the concentration of merchants and bankers gave the City of London substantial financial and political clout. In contrast to the steady momentum of the increase in the overall population, the number of inhabitants of the City declined during the eighteenth century; according to Percy's *History*[22] the City population dropped from *c.* 140,000 in 1702 to *c.* 56,000 in 1821. This might imply a decline in importance for the City. But depopulation did not detract from the City as a trading centre and it remains a vital part of the infrastructure of London.

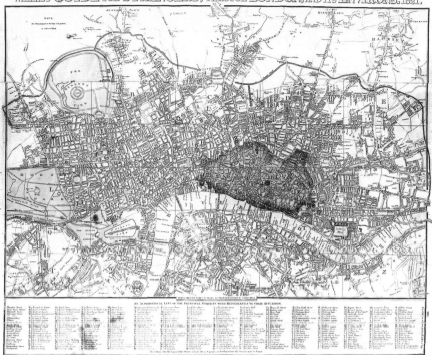

1.3 *Wallis's Guide for Strangers, through London, and its Environs, 1821*

The spread of London westwards from the early eighteenth century stretched the shape of the city and as a consequence the City of London was subsumed into the expanding geography of the metropolis (in Figure 1.3 the city is the dark, shaded area). Initially the move west was the result of the demand for better quality housing by the merchant and middle classes. And as London grew in national importance as the capital city and the centre of government and court life a house in the increasingly fashionable West End became essential for persons of *ton*. The open fields which lay to the west of Westminster were ideally situated for development. This area was owned by key aristocratic families all of whom saw the potential for short- and long-term gain in building houses. Leases on plots of land, usually for 60 years, were sold to speculative developers who produced the patchwork of terrace housing ranged around garden squares that remains the hallmark of the West End.[23] The divide between the City and the West End became ever more apparent. The modern urban infrastructure of the west outshone the medieval street pattern of the east. Moreover, the combined magnet of improved housing and a revived court life attracted the élite and their followers to the western edge of London.

This increase in the population raises the question of the different kinds of resident in the metropolis and the impact that they had on the city's growth and its infrastructure. Moreover, the composition of the population was important and goes beyond questions of birth rate and longevity. Alongside permanent residents the number of temporary residents in London, or 'town' as it was known, for the season, political or social, also increased.[24] These factors impacted on the definition of the true Londoner. Further, as the metropolis increased in physical size it is important to consider what role its new geography played in the definition of a Londoner.

The journalist and commentator on London William Hazlitt asserted that

a true cockney has never travelled beyond the purlieus of the Metropolis either in the body or in the spirit. Primrose Hill is the *Ultima Thule* of his most romantic desires; Greenwich Park stands him in good stead of the Vales of Arcady. Time and space are lost to him. He is confined to one spot and to the present moment. He sees everything near, superficial, little, in hasty succession. The world turns around and his head with it, like a roundabout at a fair, till he becomes stunned and giddy with the motion. Figures glide by as in a camera obscura.[25]

The definition of a true Londoner was then a thorny question and even as the city grew, rather like the real or virtual view from St Paul's, it remained firmly rooted in its past and London's former perimeters.

The east–west dynamic of London's infrastructure had implications for the population of the capital and represented the new demography. Old London centred around the City retained its medieval street plan and bourgeois mercantile culture. New London with its smart West End represented the new modern metropolis. But here the Crown, the aristocracy and the state were dominant, the middle classes remaining disempowered until the 1832 Reform Act. These worlds collided at Temple Bar, the traditional gated entrance to the City from the west.

Infrastructures

What then was the middle-class experience of the view of the metropolis from the top of St Paul's? What was the intricate pattern of infrastructure bound by the city's perimeter? The London streets had long proved problematical due to irrational planning which resulted in a lack of any cohesive structure and there had been several attempts to remedy it. Sir John Summerson describes the legacy of the seventeenth century:

[it] can be imagined by anybody who walks through Soho today with the object of proceeding consistently and with reasonable expedition in a given direction. Hardly

a street goes anywhere except into another street which crosses it and enforces a left or right turn. Only one street, Wardour Street (in origin a medieval field track) goes all the way through from north to south; and no street goes through from east to west.[26]

This pattern of building and feeling of disorientation is seen to be a result of small-scale building projects on tiny plots – enterprises which had no overall plan or direction. By the opening decade of the nineteenth century the direction of the main streets in London followed the Thames (Figure 1.4). There were three principal routes across London. The northernmost of the two central routes ran east–west from the Uxbridge Road to Oxford Street to Leadenhall and the Mile End Road. The southern of the two roads ran along the Bath Road, Piccadilly, Pall Mall and Charing Cross via Canon Street to the Tower of London. Neither of these could be called an axis, they were more a series of connecting roads of various widths configured in an approximate east–west direction. In both cases the road system, and beneath it the network of sewers, was subordinate to the housing and other buildings on the streets. Town planning ideas, such as they were, had concentrated on individual plots of land rather than the creation of rational infrastructures. The third route was an improvement on the latter two. Known initially as the New Road, later it became the Marylebone Road. It capped the north-western end of the city and provided an important east–west axis running in a near straight line from Paddington to Bloomsbury. This was newly built, begun in the latter half of the eighteenth century, and so was not encumbered by the existing pressures of site or street plan which characterised the former two routes.

The cross-London axes linking West End and City remained a live planning issue throughout the period. The Second Report of the Select Committee on Metropolitan Improvements in 1838 focused on opening lines of communication across the metropolis.[27] In addition to the New Road three main cross-city routes were identified and St Paul's was a focal point for them all. The first was Cumberland Gate, Oxford Street, Holborn, Skinner Street, New Gate, Cheapside and King William Street which terminated at London Bridge. The second ran south and west of Westminster to the Strand, Fleet Street, Ludgate and Cheapside. The third began at Hyde Park Corner running along Piccadilly, Coventry Street, Long Acre, Great Queen Street, Lincoln's Inn Fields through the City into Cheapside. Cheapside, which runs east from St Paul's, was the bottle neck of all these routes and a new road was proposed running from St Paul's to St Katharine's Docks to relieve it. This new road network would link the principal buildings of the City of London, including the Mansion House and the Bank of England as well as St Paul's, with those in the City of Westminster. These proposals for a direct link between the City and the West End represented the growing unification of

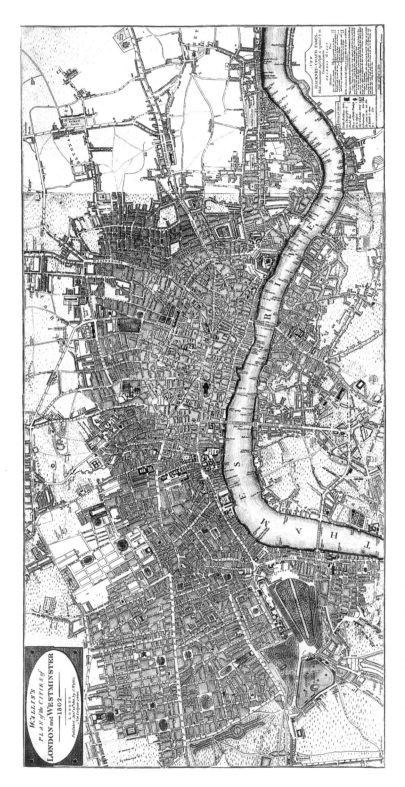

1.4   *Wallis's plan of the Cities of London and Westminster, 1802*

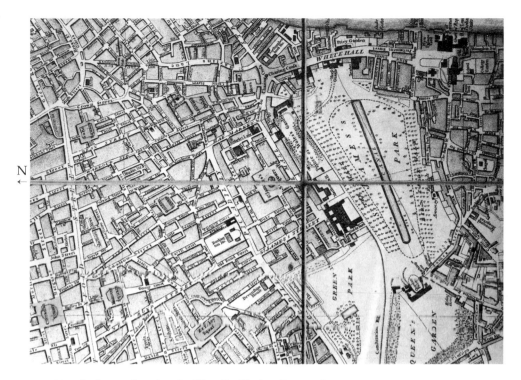

N
←

1.5   Detail of map showing the West End before Regent Street

these two previously distinctive parts of London as a bourgeois, metropolitan culture took hold in the capital in the years following the 1832 Reform Act. This stood distinct from the plans to zone London according to social class which had focused on the construction of Regent Street earlier in the nineteenth century.

The construction of the New Street from 1815, or Regent Street as it was later named, ruptured this east–west pattern of London's road network by carving a north–south axis through the centre of the Metropolis (Figure 1.5).[28] This new axis was imposed on a pre-existing street pattern rather than adhering to it. It formed the first grand route through London between the new upmarket speculative development of the Regent's Park at its north end and the ever grander royal residence, Carlton House, where it terminated at the south (Figure 1.6). George IV had inherited Carlton House when he was Prince of Wales. The structure underwent incessant alterations and renovations until it was abandoned in favour of Buckingham House in 1825 after which it was demolished. But the line of Regent Street remained an important axis and this was picked up on by the 1838 Report which proposed that the line of Waterloo Bridge be extended to Bow Street and Blackfriars to

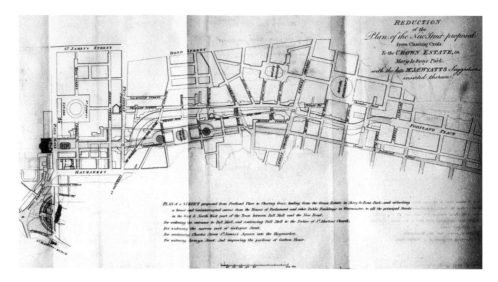

1.6   Reproduction of the plan of the New Street proposed from Charing Cross to the Crown Estate, in Mary-le-bone Park, 1815

Farringdon to allow easier circulation from north to south in the eastern half of the metropolis.

Traffic congestion was not confined to the roads. The growing importance of London as a trading centre led to an increase in river traffic and the need for more docks. The Port of London Reports of 1798 outlined unrealised plans for the improvement of the congested London Docks. This idea is taken up in *Portobello or a Plan for the improvement of the Port and City of London* drawn up by Sir Frederick Morton Eden Bart in 1798. Here the demolition of Old London Bridge is proposed to accommodate the coal or timber trade 'near the heart of the metropolis', which was seen as a far more important element in the city's infrastructure than 'a crumbling ancient structure'.

Alongside the plans to improve the London Docks a canal system to transport goods across London was part of the necessary infrastructure. The City traders provided many consumer goods and basic supplies, including fuel, for the metropolis. Once delivered to the docks goods were dispersed by road, river or canal. Canals supplemented the Thames as a major part of the transport infrastructure running, for instance, from the Isle of Dogs to Blackwall and Limehouse and to the south west of London from Dorking, Leatherhead and Walton to connect with the Thames.[29] The Regent's Canal connected the north of the Regent's Park with the east to facilitate the delivery of all manner of goods to the residents of that part of London and in no small way contributed to the enabling of the whole development.

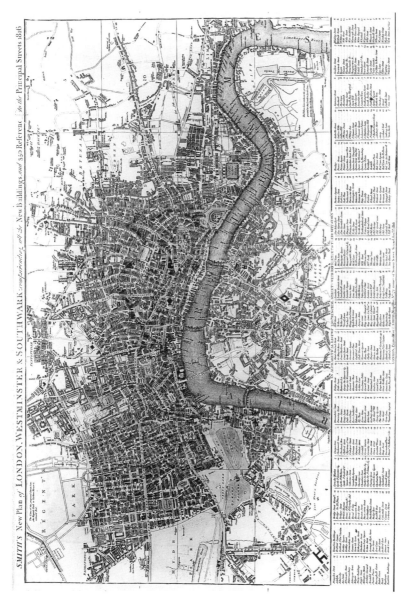

1.7 Smith's New Plan, showing Westminster, Waterloo, Vauxhall, Blackfriars and London Bridges, 1816

The increased number of bridges diminished the river's role as a physical barrier between the north and south banks. These provided new entry points into London and more effective ways of moving across the city. For instance, traffic crossing over London Bridge into Southwark could travel westwards more quickly and access the West End via Westminster Bridge. By 1820 there were five main river crossings: Westminster, Waterloo, Vauxhall and Blackfriars in the City of Westminster and Southwark and London Bridge in the City of London (Figure 1.7). As London expanded its girth so the south bank of the Thames was seen as an area with good potential for development. Not least, the open land invited the building of a rational road system. This would not only provide good communications across Southwark but also connect with the Thames bridges.

Residential and commercial areas were being developed away from the Thames. And the improved network of roads, canals and bridges permitted travel and circulation across and through the metropolis by a variety of means. This created a new spatial map of the urban environment and new kinds of experience of the city.

The relationship of the infrastructure to the perimeter and the new image of London comes to the fore at its edges or entrance points. These became increasingly significant in the period. Perhaps influenced by Ledoux's barriers in Paris they became benchmarks of metropolitan greatness and hegemony. Two entrances, visible from the real or virtual St Paul's panorama, were developed and built over a similar time period. Both begun in 1823, they exemplify how the new metropolis was laid over the old and aspects of the old city reconfigured to embellish the image and status of the new. They were Hyde Park Corner in the developing West End and the rebuilding of London Bridge in the City.

Entering the 'new' metropolis: the importance of Hyde Park Corner

Hyde Park Corner had traditionally been the main entrance into London from the west (Figure 1.8) and during the eighteenth century there had been plans to develop it into a monumental entrance way. The idea may have developed out of John Gwynn's proposal in his *London and Westminster Improved* (1766) for a *Place* at Hyde Park Corner from which main avenues radiated. Gwynn felt the area needed improvement as it was so close to the royal residences. His idea was developed further in 1778 by Robert Adam who designed a monumental gateway. This plan may well have evolved during the time Adam was designing and building the terrace of brick townhouses at Hyde Park Corner (1771–8). (Apsley House was the most westward of these and had the address No 1 London.) It comprised an

1.8   Thomas Shotter Boys, View of Hyde Park Corner showing Decimus Burton's screen and arch

archway flanked on either side by entrances into the two royal parks. The nationalistic overtones of such a monument rendered the plan impractical on financial and ideological grounds. Britain had lost a valuable colony in the expensive American War of Independence and the subsequent economic gloom and subdued national mood made this an inappropriate moment for extravagant celebration. The idea was revived by Jeffery Wyatt who exhibited a scheme at the Royal Academy in 1791 and a monumental gateway was planned by George III.[30] Four years later Soane, on his appointment as architect to the Office of Woods, provided plans for improvements in the parks including, at the behest of George III, a monumental entrance way to Hyde Park from Piccadilly and an entrance into Green Park. Soane's plans also included a new royal palace in the northwest corner of Green Park. Other architects presented plans for the site including William Kinnaird who in 1813 published 'View of a Triumphal Arch, Proposed To Be Erected at Hyde Park Corner, commemorative of the victories achieved by British Arms during the Reign of His Majesty King George the Third'.[31] None of these plans was executed.[32]

So Hyde Park Corner already had great significance for the capital and was seen as the gateway into London. The recent victories over the French at Trafalgar and Waterloo had created the need for adequate commemoration of the nation's war heroes. A fund of £300,000 had been set up by Parliament in 1816 for the erection of commemorative monuments. Perhaps in response to this, in 1817 Soane presented another scheme for Hyde Park Corner which he exhibited at the Royal Academy and which followed Adam's design of an archway running across Piccadilly with decorative sculpture commemorating the two battles.[33] But once again no action was taken.

In 1823 Decimus Burton was brought in to design an entrance into Hyde Park, known as the Hyde Park Screen. The park had become increasingly important and was the scene of national celebrations and a favoured haunt of the flâneur/euse. The Hyde Park Screen provided the monarch with a ceremonial entrance into this royal park. Significantly, it was placed at a 90° angle to the junction of Piccadilly and Knightsbridge, the road coming in from the west, so making the long planned construction of an entrance to London across Piccadilly virtually impossible. The meaning of Hyde Park Corner was changed further by the decision in the 1820s to demolish Carlton House, the home of George IV, and to develop Buckingham House, situated at the end of The Mall at the junction of Green Park and St James's Park, into a new royal palace. This not only altered the shape and orientation of the plan for a new London but also transformed Hyde Park Corner from an entrance into London and a symbol of the metropolis to a signifier of national and Hanoverian greatness. Hyde Park now abutted the back garden of the new royal residence and this helped to attract the crowds of aristocratic and bourgeois metropolitan residents who paraded about the walks and rides of the parks. A ceremonial entrance was needed to allow the monarch to process from his new palace into the park under the gaze of his subjects. To this end a second arch was proposed, known initially as the Green Park Arch but later called the Arch at Constitution Hill as it stood at the beginning of this route through Green Park to St James's Park. The second arch was aligned with the Hyde Park Screen to provide a fitting, monumental entrance way for the king into Hyde Park, the scene of military parades and mock battles. This meant that the traditional gateway into London from the west at the end of Piccadilly was now irreversibly turned 90° to align with Buckingham Palace. Both arches were to be decorated with sculptural celebrations of Britain's military victories, intellectual prowess and the Hanoverian dynasty. And the emphasis in this western edge of London changed from a symbol of the metropolis to the representation of nation and state.[34]

Those entering London from the west would now pass between the two gateways instead of proceeding through at least one of them. This is shown in a photograph of a painting by James Holland showing Hyde Park Corner in 1827.[35] The missed opportunity of a gateway into London is picked up by the *Mechanics' Magazine* in 1827 which stated that the reorientation of the area had robbed London of its best opportunity for a monumental entrance to the city. Moreover as London was extending at a substantial rate there was now a deficiency in the grandeur of the approaches to the British metropolis. The magazine commented at length on the Hyde Park Screen:

When the present peace left the English at leisure to turn their attention to internal improvements the erection of a grand triumphal entrance to the metropolis, similar to the Propylaea of Athens, was among the first things contemplated. Several designs were offered to the Government for the purpose; and an understanding came generally to prevail, that such a structure would certainly be erected at Hyde Park Corner. According to the idea which most people formed of the projected building it was to be erected at the summit of the assent from Knightsbridge, and to embrace the whole width of the road, having side entrances to Hyde Park and Green Park, nor can there be a question, that a structure like the Propylaea, erected in such a situation, would have had a most magnificent and imposing effect. To the everlasting discredit, however, of the spirit amid taste which preside over like architectural improvements of this auspicious era, our long talked of 'triumphal entrance' has divided into a mere Park entrance, which, like the Palace leaves us where we were before without that important addition to the metropolis so fondly anticipated and so much wanted.[36]

The opening up of Hyde Park Corner and the removal of the toll gates enabled the further spread of London as Percy's *History* noted: 'London continued spreading during the long war and peace has given new impetus to this except in the west where Hyde Park Corner is a stopping block.'[37] It also facilitated the creation of a new kind of social urban space where the residents of London became both viewers and the viewed.

Entering 'old' London: the rebuilding of London Bridge

The westward growth of London had largely been confined to the north bank of the Thames. The common aspect of all the circulatory patterns so far discussed was that they did not need to cross the river. But this did not necessarily diminish the role of the river as an important part in the metropolitan infrastructure. It remained not only a vital transport link between the two ends of the metropolis and an effective means of transporting goods but also a barrier that had to be crossed to enter the capital – especially the City of London. The importance of bridges as entrances to the metropolis is undeniable and more visitors entered London by crossing the Thames than by passing through Hyde Park Corner. But the bridges rarely received much aesthetic attention. This was remarked upon by the editor of the *Mechanics' Magazine*:

May I venture to hope that, since Hyde Park Corner has lost the honour designed for it, and since a triumphal entrance into London is a thing still to be accomplished, the claims of Waterloo Bridge to the distinction will yet receive the consideration they merit? Or should its [triumphal entrance] erection on that spot be now inconvenient, would not the opening of the approaches to the New London Bridge furnish an excellent opportunity for adding so noble a monument to the metropolis?[38]

London Bridge was the first bridge across the Thames and the structure dated from medieval times. It remained one of the principal entrances into London and came increasingly to represent the identity of the City as distinct from the metropolis as a whole.[39] Yet it was an important part of the urban infrastructure being, for most of the eighteenth century, one of only three ways of accessing the northern bank of the Thames from the south side of the river, the others being Westminster Bridge, begun in the late 1730s, and Blackfriars, begun in 1760. These bridges formed 'a great trio of supra aquatic streets' according to J. P. Malcolm.[40]

By the mid-eighteenth century Old London Bridge had undergone many necessary repairs and alterations. The old houses which were remnants of the medieval bridge were removed in 1759 and the centre arch rebuilt by the Corporation of London's architects Robert Taylor and George Dance the elder in the same year. This went some way towards improving the bridge's appearance and reducing the adverse effect on tidal flows. Although the widened central arch also allowed more river traffic which improved trade, these efforts were not enough. The first moves to completely redevelop the bridge and the surrounding area came at the end of the eighteenth century as part of the Port of London improvements.[41] Various new bridge designs were drawn up between 1799 and 1801 including Dance the younger's ambitious proposal which would have more than matched the grandeur of the Metropolitan Improvements in the West End. By contrast the surveyor Thomas Telford proposed that Old London Bridge be replaced by a cast iron single span. This was a very different but equally potent symbol of metropolitan modernity. Attention turned again to the state of Old London Bridge in 1821 when the engineer John Rennie, who had worked on both Waterloo and Southwark Bridges, argued that further repairs and alterations would cost as much as a new structure. The Corporation of London acted on Rennie's advice and sought an Act of Parliament to allow them to replace the bridge. (Figure 1.9).[42]

The self-conscious attempt to develop London into a world class city as seen in the Metropolitan Improvements had implications for the work at London Bridge. Regent Street, the Regent's Park, the new Royal Palace and Royal Parks, and not least the monumental entrance way into the metropolis from the west at Hyde Park Corner had or were beginning to transform the image of London from what Sir John Summerson described as a 'huddle of

1.9   View of New London Bridge, 1829

bricks with a steepled skyline' into a world class city. These improvements were being orchestrated and overseen by the Offices of Woods and Works – agents of the Crown who were answerable to parliament and who were largely funded by the public purse. Here the responsibility for the work and the initial cost of the entire project fell to the Corporation of London, an autonomous body concerned with the local government of the City. The Act of Parliament that gave the City of London permission to replace London Bridge brought with it some financial support for the project.[43]

According to R. L. Jones, a member of the Bridge House Committee which oversaw the work, this was appropriate as the bridge 'was one of great and important public character', and the committee 'might fairly look to the Government for support and assistance'.[44] Despite its financial support the government did not get involved with the competition for the design of the new bridge which was held in 1823. But there were conditions which aligned the rebuilding of London Bridge to other parts of the Metropolitan Improvements. Like Hyde Park Corner and other projects belonging to the improvements the width of the road was to be increased together with the quality of its surface and steepness of its gradient. The rubric for the competition included that the bridge be faced with granite that there should be five arches and that the centre arch should be 23 feet above water level. The new structure should be erected no more than 70 feet west of the present (old) bridge with these instructions:

It is desirable that the bridge should be worthy of the metropolis and the present cultivated state of science, due regard being had at the same time to Economy and convenience of traffic over and under the bridge during the progress and after completion of the works.

But the design should allow 'formation of the necessary approaches as is consistent with the character of so important an entrance to the city of London'. The competition was a failure, producing designs from architects of the second rank and a loud furore over the way in which the whole affair had been managed.[45]

Attention turned again to the architecturally austere functional design offered by John Rennie. This was executed by John Rennie junior as his father had died in 1821. This plan proposed that the new bridge be built on the exact site of the old one and elevated at either end to correspond with the level of the old approaches.

The Bridge House Committee recommended that the bridge be moved 180 feet west of the old one so avoiding the steep hill of Fish Street. The width of the bridge had been increased by 6 feet on Rennie's original scheme in the interest of greater public convenience and to accommodate the expected increase in traffic. This would, however, render 'new, more commodious, and much more expensive approaches necessary'. But the revised scheme would provide a fitting entrance into the City from the Southwark side of the river. Moreover, as attention turned increasingly to thoroughfares through London, London Bridge was seen as connecting with roads on either sides of the river and creating a continuous route across the city.

As the bridge neared completion in 1829 the Corporation of London presented to parliament designs for the bridge approaches from the south. A variety of plans were put forward as a supplement to Rennie's original intentions for the approaches. These included designs from better known architects than had been involved with the bridge competition, including C.R. Cockerell, Robert Smirke and his pupil Henry Roberts.[46] Both Cockerell's and Roberts' designs provide an adequate response to the urban vision of the Metropolitan Improvements. But the work was given to Robert Smirke about whom it was remarked '[of Smirke's] undoubted purity of taste (we wish we could add fertility of invention) much is to be hoped'.[47] Less generously Cockerell lamented Smirke's embellishment of the London Bridge approaches remarking that 'a more unworthy set of buildings was never designed'.

Attention was also paid to the north bank of the Thames where the bridge entered the City. Here several schemes were put forward for a grand square or place incorporating the Monument which remained a symbol of the City's re-emergence after the Great Fire. In an unusual case of urban symmetry one such proposal came from James Burton, a very successful property developer and the father of the architect Decimus, who was working on Hyde Park Corner. Burton senior's unexpected design was for a triumphal arch set in a circus.[48]

Notes

1. For a discussion of the status of domed buildings as *axis mundi* see Yi Fu Tuan, *Topophilia*, Englewood Cliffs, NJ, Prentice Hall, 1974, 169–70 esp.

2. Robert Mudie, *Babylon the Great*, London, 1825.

3. The Colosseum was designed by Decimus Burton for Thomas Hornor. The design was based on the Pantheon, rather than its Roman namesake, but was polygonal instead of circular. There was already a building known as The Pantheon at Oxford Circus but the nomenclature continued the augustan image of London. It measured 130 feet in diameter with a giant portico and large cupola. Full details of its planning and construction can be found in PRO Cres 2/777.

4. It was changed into a concert hall in 1831 and was demolished in 1875.

5. *Mechanics' Magazine*, 6(155), Saturday 12 August 1826, 225ff.

6. T. Hornor, *Views of London from the observatory over the cross of St Paul's, Four engravings by T. Hornor*, London, 1822.

7. M. Foucault, *The Order of Things. an archaeology of human sciences*, London, Tavistock, 1970.

8. This idea has been explored by several feminist writers on the city. See E. Wilson, 'The Invisible Flâneur', *New Left Review*, 191, 1992, 90–110; J. Wolff, 'The Invisible Flâneuse: women and the literature of modernity', *Feminine Sentences: Essays on Women Culture and Modernity*, Oxford, Polity Press, 1990, 34–50.

9. *Serveiller* is usually translated as discipline.

10. M. Foucault, *Discipline and Punish (Surveiller et Punir)*, London, Penguin, 1979.

11. On this point see R. Altick, *The Shows of London*, Cambridge, Mass., Harvard University Press, 1978, 180 esp.

12. The privileging of vision over other senses has constructed a way of seeing which is predominantly male. In this context sight, vision or views of the metropolis can present a skewed analysis of the experience of the city by men and women. This issue is fully discussed by Doreen Massey, 'Flexible Sexism', *Society and Space*, 9(1), 1991, 45 esp.

13. Robert Southey, *Letters from England*, 1807.

14. B. Lambert, *The History and Survey of London*, 4 vols, London, 1806.

15. E. M. Butler (ed.) *A Regency Visitor, The English Tour of Prince Pückler-Muskau Described in his letters 1826–1828*, London, Collins, 1957, letter dated 8 April 1827, 189.

16. Ibid., 190.

17. S. and R. Percy, *The Percy History and Interesting memorial on the rise, progress and present state of all the capitals of Europe*, 3 vols, London, 1823, vol. III, 353.

18. E. M. Butler *op. cit.*, 189.

19. For a discussion of the developing relationship between London and its suburbs in the eighteenth century see E. McKellar, 'Peripheral Visions: alternative aspects and rural presences in mid-eighteenth century London' in D. Arnold (ed.) *The Metropolis and its Image: constructing identities for London 1750–1950*, Oxford, The Association of Art Historians and Blackwell, 1999

20. B. Lambert, *History and Survey of London*, 1806, 536.

21. Summerson *op. cit.* (n. 23) states that the population of London was 674,500 in 1700, increasing to 676,750 by 1750, but cites no source for these figures.

22. S. and R. Percy *op. cit.*

23. For a fuller discussion of the building of the West End see J. Summerson, *Georgian London*, Harmondsworth, Penguin, 1978

24. For a discussion of the relationship between town house and country house see M. H. Port, 'Town House and Country House: their interaction' in D. Arnold, *The Georgian Country House: architecture, landscape and society*, Stroud and New York, Sutton Publishing, 1998, 117–38.

25. William Hazlitt, 'On Londoners and Country People', *New Monthly Magazine*, August 1823.

26. J. Summerson, *The Life and Work of John Nash, Architect*, Cambridge, Mass. and London, MIT, 1980, 75.

27. Parliamentary Papers 1837–8 XVI 661.

28. See J. Summerson, *op. cit.* (n. 26) for a discussion of the substantial role played by John Nash in the building of Regent Street.

29. See Revd Henry Hunter, *History of London and its environs*, 2 vols, 1811, 1, xiv and xvii.

30. George III's set of drawings are held at the British Museum, King's maps xxvii 26 a–c.

31. Copies of this engraving exist in the British Museum, King's Maps xxviii and the Bodleian Library (Douce Prints N. 8).

32. See D. Stroud, 'Hyde Park Corner', *Architectural Review*, 106, 1949, 379–97.

33. These plans are illustrated in John Soane, *Designs for Public and Private Buildings*, London, 1828.

34. For a full discussion of the development of Hyde Park Corner at this time and the evolution of the designs for both the Hyde Park Screen and the Arch at Constitution Hill see D. Arnold, 'The Arch at Constitution Hill: a new axis for London', *Apollo*, CXXXVIII (379), September 1993, 129–33.

35. At least two prints of this image exist. One is held at the Victoria and Albert Museum and is not accessioned but can be found in box no. A149a. A version of the photograph is also in a private collection.

36. *Mechanics' Magazine*, VIII (208), 18 August 1827, 65ff.

37. S. and R Percy *op. cit.*, III, 353.

38. *Mechanics' Magazine*, VIII (208), 18 August 1827, 65ff.

39. For a full discussion of this see D. Arnold, 'London Bridge and its Symbolic Identity in the Regency Metropolis: the dialectic of civic and national pride' in D. Arnold (ed.) *The Metropolis and its Image: constructing identities for London c.1750–1950*, Oxford, the Association of Art Historians and Blackwell, 1999, 79–100.

40. J. P. Malcolm, *London Redivivium*, 1, 1803, 385.

41. The Third Report from the Select Committee upon the Improvements of the Port of London was published in 1801.

42. Rennie's report was submitted on 12 March 1821. The original specification for the new bridge is held in the University of London Library MS. 158. Rennie died in October the same year.

43. Most of the new bridges across the Thames were built by private companies which speculated on the profits from tolls. But government funding was forthcoming for the rebuilding of London Bridge most likely because of the symbiotic nature of the cities of London and Westminster and in recognition of the symbolic potential of London Bridge as an image of a modern metropolis. The government granted £150,000 to be raised by taxes. Chief amongst these was the coal tax levied at 8d. per ton for coal brought to the City for sale by land or through the Port of London. 10 Geo. IV, c. 136 and 11 Geo. IV, c. 64.

44. R. L. Jones, *Reminiscences of the Public Life of Richard Lambert Jones Esq.*, London, 1863.

45. On this point see Arnold, 1999 *op. cit.* and the catalogue for the New London Bridge Competition Exhibition held in 1823 in Sir John Soane's Museum, PC 55/2; *A professional survey of Old and New London Bridges and their approaches*, 1831. Soane Museum PC 23/4 and I. Andrews, *London Bridge and No New Taxes*, London, 1823.

46. Several drawings exist which relate to the scheme. The following are held in the Yale Center for British Art, Paul Mellon Collection: C. R. Cockerell, Design for the Approaches to London Bridge, B1975.2.632; H. Roberts, Design for the Approaches to London Bridge, B1975.2.635.

47. Soane Museum PC 23/4, p. 43.

48. *Mechanics' Magazine*, XVI (427), 15 October 1831, 40.

2

The Art of Walking the Streets

In John Britton's description of the Colosseum the panorama was said to give 'a view of the British Metropolis without parallel'.[1] Most impressive of all were the two viewpoints of London offered to the visitor: one from above and the other at street level. The bird's-eye view was just that – a view – where the optical experience of the city and its shape remained dominant. But the abstract patchwork of shapes and patterns which comprised the infrastructure of London were the actual streets and squares surrounding the Colosseum, which offered a different more varied sensory experience when encountered at ground level. Public spaces and the growing importance of public life also played their part in the way urban culture developed at this time. In this way the anonymous, genderless gaze of the viewer from the top of St Paul's was transformed into the flâneur and the flâneuse[2] whose detached dislocated lonely experience of the city encompassed more senses than just sight.[3] The spectacle of Parisian life, as articulated by Charles Baudelaire, might be where the languid figure of the flâneur/euse sought novelty and entertainment. But this practice of viewing and yet being disengaged from the processes of urban life had its roots in the dilettanti and dandies of early nineteenth-century London. In one way the trope of flânerie indicates a similar kind of scopic regime to the panopticon but the emphasis on mobility and fluidity ensures it remains a distinct practice. The differences in viewing the city between the panopticon of the Colosseum and the flâneurie of the experience of the streets were identified and connected by Walter Benjamin who remarked, 'The city-dweller … attempts to introduce the countryside into the city. In the panoramas the city dilates to become landscape, as it does in a subtler way for the flâneur.'[4]

If the flâneur is a construct of the post-Napoleonic period in France, used to represent the modernity of Paris, it might well appear that there is little connection to early nineteenth-century London. But there was a constant cultural, social and architectural dialogue between the two cities. There is no doubt that the years 1800–1840 witnessed the birth of a modern metropolis and the first city of the British Empire. Paris was seen as the immediate competition and George IV is reported as declaring that 'the splendours of Napoleon's Paris would be eclipsed by what he planned for London'.[5] On his visits to Paris in 1814 and 1815 the monarch's principal architect John Nash was certainly impressed by Napoleon I's creation of the straight rue du Rivoli with its classical arcades and mixture of shops and housing. This must only have confirmed the decision he had made a few years earlier to base the Regent Street development – the apogee of bourgeois urban planning – on such a continental model. But the flow of ideas was reversed in the Paris of Louis Philippe and the second Empire which drew inspiration from the London of George IV particularly in terms of its urban planning of streets and parks which helped shape urban experience.[6] Frequent references to Paris were made in the writings about London. And these comparisons of the two cities in terms of their similarities and differences were encouraged on both sides of the Channel. There was general agreement that both capitals were impressive but for different reasons. This opinion is typified by a French guidebook which commented, 'Londres, malgré son étendue, sa population et ses richesses, ne présente pas à l'admiration des étrangers, autant de beaux édifices publics et particuliers, que plusieurs des principales villes de l'Europe.'[7] (In spite of its size, population and wealth London does not offer the visitor as many beautiful public and private buildings as several of the major European cities.) But the authors conceded that the cities were equally magnificent in their overall effect. This view of London was echoed in indigenous guidebooks. Darton's *Description of London* (1824) noted that 'London does not excel other great cities ... in the grandeur and beauty of its buildings', but the developments in the upmarket western half of the metropolis did not go unnoticed as Darton remarked: 'it has recently undergone some magnificent improvements at the western extremity'.[8]

The emergence of a new bourgeois metropolitan personality which found expression in the architecture and street life of London – especially the West End – means the concept of the flâneur/euse is an effective way of examining the social and cultural modernity of the metropolis. Male and female experience of the London streets did differ, however. The flâneur or anonymous male viewer had greater freedom to roam the streets and visit the clubs and other places of public entertainment and edification which proliferated in this period. This was a new kind of public persona and the urban form of London both responded to and helped create this new class of citizen. The increased prominence of public life also redefined the presence of women in the urban cityscape. Previously a 'public' woman was a prostitute and her presence on the streets was a statement of her trade. But in the new social arena of the early nineteenth-century city the middle and upper middle class occupants' patterns of life changed this associative relationship between women and the streets. The increasing appearance of 'respectable' women in public spaces, albeit heavily chaperoned, meant there was a flâneuse in early nineteenth-century London and she visited and was seen in the public parks, shopping arcades and garden squares. Indeed pleasure grounds were constructed in the Royal Parks with the idea of encouraging women and children to enjoy the open spaces and benefits of the fresh air. In this way the flâneuse's gendered sensory experience of the city was as visible and invisible as the male.

The idea of exploring the city and experiencing urban street life is not, however, confined to the nineteenth century. Right at the beginning of the eighteenth century John Gay, in his mock georgic poem *Trivia* (literally *The Streets* in Latin) which was subtitled *The Art of Walking the Streets* (1716), discussed 'Of walking the Streets by Day' and 'Of Walking the Streets by Night' in books II and III respectively. Gay presents the tangled knot of the street plan of the old city around Seven Dials in Covent Garden as a labyrinth where his flâneur is disorientated if not lost

> Bewildered, trudges on from place to place;
> he dwells on ev'ry sign, with stupid gaze,
> Enters the narrow alley's doubtful maze,
> tries ev'ry winding court and street in vain,
> And doubles o'er his weary steps again.
> Thus hardly Theseus, with intrepid feet,
> Traversed the dang'rous labyrinth of Crete
> (*Trivia*, II. 78–84)

The confusing plan of the city and its dangers – both moral and physical – only intensify as night falls.

The immeasurability of a city and the idea of it being a labyrinth prompted new ways of conceptualising the city which sometimes resulted in it being brought onto a human scale in order to express it in terms of the human body, human language or human art. This kind of imagery enables an exploration of the energies that bring human beings together and attempts to harness them in the interests of social life. This prompts the need to balance an individual's private life and a social public existence and our need to share. Different levels of existence and experience within the city found a variety of expressions. For many writers London had a force humankind could not control or order, which went beyond physical experience and encompassed all the senses. The community of natural forms Wordsworth found in his description of Bartholomew Fair in *The Prelude* 'monstrous in colour, motion, shape, sight and sound' embodies the sensory diversity of urban experience and echoes Hazlitt's description of the experience of a 'true cockney' in its kaleidoscopic vision.[9]

The flow of human existence through the streets and squares of London remains a potent image of the experience of resident and visitor alike. Gay had recognised the confused and confusing nature of the London street plan in the early eighteenth century which only received some remedial attention in the opening decades of the nineteenth century. The abstract qualities of civic space were also recognised by Daniel Defoe who described a journey made by Moll Flanders across the city without any tactile or visual reference where London becomes a network of streets and connections 'into Long-Lane so away into Charterhouse-Yard and out onto St John's Street, then across into Smithfield'.[10] The labyrinthine, irrational medieval street plan of the City referred to here by Defoe in the 1720s endured into the early nine-teenth century and even where buildings and areas had been renewed its imprint remained. Indeed S. E. Rasmussen recognised this in his description of London:

The English square or crescent ... is a restricted whole as complete as the courtyard of a convent. They form fine geometrical figures in the town plan, they are regular and completely uniform on all sides, and a series of such squares may be linked together in any order ... It is as if the traditions of the Middle Ages had been handed down to the present day in the squares in these domestic quarters. But the narrow courts of the old town have been transformed into the open squares of the newer quarters.[11]

The city was then in a state of flux and the motion of the streets was an essential part of urban experience. Buildings and monuments positioned in the cityscape had a separate existence and the importance of vista and ap-proach became increasingly important as an urban self-consciousness evolved. These fragments were indeed the hallmark of modern urban life. Here there was no such thing as a complete narrative. Instead the populace and visitors brushed against each other to see excerpts from other lives and it is in this context that the marginal and dislocated flâneur/euse emerges. The public parks were ideal locations for such encounters as *The Picture of London* noted in 1802: 'numbers of people of fashion mingled with a great multitude of well dressed people of various ranks'. The volume of visitors to the parks was considerable; up to 100,000 took the air in Kensington Palace Gardens and Hyde Park at any one time (Figure 2.1). The most particular displays of opulence took place between 2 and 5 pm. This voyeuristic aspect of social interchange was underscored by the guidebook which recommended that the visitor stop to take in the whole scene of horsemen, landscape and walkers and even advised that the Broad Walk at the foot of the basin of the Serpentine offered the best vantage point.[12] But there were restrictions on the

2.1   Thomas Shotter Boys, View of Hyde Park, near Grosvenor Gate. Coloured tinted lithograph

(viewing) public who entered this space. No servants in livery or women with pattens[13] were admitted during the official opening hours of 8 am to 8 pm. Needless to say the parks took on a very different character after dark. But public promenades were enjoyed by all classes and dress did not necessarily betray rank: 'all ranks of females display a lightness of drapery which would completely characterize the dimensions of a Grecian statue'.[14]

These fragmentary encounters in the newly defined urban streets and parks reveal the discontinuities of modernity where feelings of melancholy and isolation come to the fore. The flâneur/euse experienced feelings of nostalgia and loss for lives unknown and experiences that can only be guessed at. Thomas de Quincey's *Confessions of an Opium Eater* (1821) is an autobiographical account of the melancholy of a young man in London. De Quincey uses the 'mighty labyrinth of London' to give a vivid portrayal of his character's feeling of marginality and isolation when he searches for his lost love – a prostitute or 'public' woman – on the city's streets. The ebb and flow of the crowds is evoked in phrases describing Oxford Street as 'the great Mediterranean' which 'echoed the groans of innumerable hearts'. De Quincey's recognition of the anonymity of metropolitan life was picked up on by later writers including Poe and Charles Baudelaire, who translated his work into French. The marginalised outsider on the streets of London became part of the ongoing cultural dialogue around the conceptualisation of urban space between London and Paris in the nineteenth century. The resonance between the two capitals continues with de Quincey's writings on *The*

Nation of London (1834) where the description of the emotional response to the city is not dissimilar to that of Baudelaire's flâneur:

These are feelings that do not belong by preference to thoughtful people – far less to people merely sentimental. No man ever was left to himself for the first time in the streets, as yet unknown, of London, but he must have been saddened and mortified, perhaps terrified, by the sense of desertion and utter loneliness which belong to his situation. No loneliness can be like that which weighs upon the heart in the centre of faces never-ending, without voice or utterance for him; eyes innumerable, that have 'no speculation' in their orbs which *he* can understand; and hurrying figures of man and women weaving to and fro, with no apparent purposes intelligible to a stranger, seeming like a mask of maniacs, or, oftentimes, like a pageant of phantoms.[15]

Urban isolation and its consequences for the emotions was a popular image of the modern metropolis. Hazlitt remarked on this in his comments on the differences between the country and the city in *The Plain Speaker* (1826):

It is a strange state of society (such as that in London) where a man does not know his next-door neighbour, and where the feelings (one would think) must recoil upon themselves, and either fester or become obtuse.

The urban scene becomes a modern utopia and dystopia at the same time.[16] In this way the metropolis presented itself as a set of various social and symbolic spaces which were negotiated, interpreted and improvised upon by its range of publics. Henri Lefebvre identified this kind of physical envi-ronment as a 'representational space'[17] which provided 'an "anthropological", poetic and mythical experience'.[18] The early nineteenth-century flâneur/ euse encountered this virtual and actual city through its street pattern and its society. But how was the gaze of the resident or visitor to be directed through this self-consciously constructed urban landscape?

Reading the city

There were a variety of ways in which the city could be seen, moved through and experienced. The guidebook or history played an important part in promoting this public consumption of the metropolis. But there were other sorts of urban narratives which told of a different kind of urban experience. Pierce Egan's *Life in London: the Day and Night Scenes of Jerry Hawthorn Esq. and his elegant friend Corinthian Tom, accompanied by Bob Logic, the Oxonian, in their Rambles and Sprees through the Metropolis* (1821) typifies this kind of urban writing. Moreover by drawing on established literary traditions most notably the picaresque novel and the pairing of a worldly wise (urban) character with a naïve (country) tourist the text demonstrates how the early modern city informed the representation of its early nineteenth-century coun-terpart. The adventures of the two flâneurs was published in monthly

2.2 The Grand Lounge; Regent Street to wit, Tom and his party off to the Races; Jerry bowing to Kate and Sue, 1821

instalments accompanied by illustrations from the brothers Cruikshank. The metropolis is portrayed as a variety of visual experiences which are on offer round the clock and the pair, in a parody of the Grand Tour (accompanied by Logic – a kind of Bear Leader), enjoy the sights with the touristic gaze of the bourgeoisie. The flâneurie of the London street scene is ably captured by the Cruikshanks' illustrations (Figure 2.2), but the panoptic mode of viewing is not forgotten. Indeed a working example of Bentham's 'seeing machine' is visited by the threesome who are impressed: 'On ascending to the top of Newgate [prison], the TRIO expressed themselves much pleased, on looking down into the different yards, and witnessing the excellent mode of discipline'.[19] The sense of control over the lower orders and consequent feeling of security expressed here through the medium of the 'discipline' of the panopticon is a strong theme in the text. The trio's observations of the lower orders, often living in straitened circumstances, appear callous to today's reader. But their disengaged viewing practices represent how the distanced urban panorama gave the bourgeoisie a feeling of empowerment and security and distracted them from their own position in relation to the 'discipline' of the metropolis.

Egan's *Life in London* stood outside the paradigm of the guidebook. But both kinds of texts encouraged exploration of the streets – especially on foot.

The proliferation of guidebooks, many of which were republished several times in the opening years of the nineteenth century, betray how the metropolis began to be seen as a self-consciously constructed artefact with a recognised process for viewing. These guidebooks included *The Ambulator*, Leigh's *New Picture of London* and *The Picture of London*. These texts were divided up according to geographical area and encouraged perambulations around the metropolis and its suburbs, streets and squares. The *Ambulator* even provided a map covering 25 square miles.

There were other ways of exploring the metropolis as seen in J. B. B. Barjaud and C. P. Landon's *Description de Londres et de ses environs* (Paris, 1810). The authors' intention was to offer a way of comparing these two major capitals. They had completed a guidebook to Paris and used the same way of presenting the city to allow the fullest possible comparison. In this way rather than a street by street exploration a brief sketch of the city was followed by a systemised discussion of building types beginning with churches then public buildings, palaces and so forth. Quite clearly London lacked many of the grand edifices so evident in Paris.[20] This was recognised by many guidebook commentators. In response to this, more abstract qualities of London were brought to the fore and were seen to equal the aesthetic appeal of Paris, showing that there were different ways of seeing and experiencing the city. *The Ambulator*, in its tenth edition by 1811, remarked 'Some squares and streets in the metropolis are magnificent and many of those which cannot boast grandeur are long, spacious and airy.'[21]

Alongside the guidebooks, histories of London such as B. Lambert's *The History and Survey of London* (4 vols, 1806) and S. and R. Percy's *The Percy History and Interesting memorial on the rise, progress and present state of all the capitals of Europe* (3 vols, 1823) proliferated. These were lengthy, detailed accounts of the metropolis from Roman times which prompted an appreciation of the capital on a variety of social and cultural levels. Maps and plans of the metropolis were also mass produced for general consumption. The Tallis maps and Mog's *New Plan of the Cities of London and Westminster* offered a new kind of empowerment as the city became a visually legible artefact. The different authorial voices of the narrative of the city and the variety of ways in which it could be explored made an understanding of the metropolis more attainable to a wider range of publics. But the legibility of the text of the city made it at once more accessible and yet more complex as an artefact.

The opaque city

The Ambulator's description of the 'airy' London streets was at best an optimistic one. The use of coal as the principal fuel in the metropolis had a

A PEEP AT THE GAS LIGHTS IN PALL MALL.

2.3   George Moutard Woodward and Thomas Rowlandson, *A Peep at the Gas Lights in Pall-Mall,* 1809. Etching, partly coloured

damaging effect on its atmosphere. From the seventeenth century the soot-laden air had been the subject of criticism for its inhibiting effect on urban life and city dwellers' health. John Evelyn called it 'that Hellish and dismall cloud of sea-coale'.[22] But there was little else with which to fuel the growing metropolis. By the early nineteenth century the pall of soot-infested cloud grew ever worse. The popularity of the season kept the beau monde in town during the colder months which meant more coal fires and more pollution. By 1813 atmospheric conditions had declined to such an extent that a fog descended on 27 December not to lift until 3 January of the following year. The city ground to a standstill and the residents experienced a sensation of disorientation from their familiar surroundings. Dickens' description of a similar fog in *Bleak House* (1853) evokes this feeling of dislocation:

Fog everywhere. … Chance people on the bridges peeping over the parapets into a nether sky of fog, with fog all around them, as if they were up in a balloon, and hanging in the misty clouds.

Ironically the enthusiasm for street lighting helped create this problem of urban opacity. Gas lighting, fuelled by gas manufactured from coal, was first demonstrated in London in 1807 by Frederick Winsor who lit up Pall Mall in honour of the Prince Regent's birthday (Figure 2.3). This syncophantic act by the Moravian émigré was so successful that the Regent actively encouraged the introduction of gas lighting. No doubt the possibility of the impressive new modern metropolis on view at all times of the day and night was an irresistible prospect. The more practical application of its use as a deterrent to street crime must have enhanced its allure. The Gas-Light and Coke Co. was set up in 1812 to provide light for the cities of London, Westminster and the Borough of Southwark. Westminster Bridge was amongst the first major public edifices to be illuminated and street lights quickly appeared all over London. Byron picks up on this in his description of Don Juan's return to London:[23]

> The Lamps of Westminster's more regular gleam,
> The breadth of pavement, and yon shrine where fame is
> A spectral resident – whose pallid beam
> In shape of moonshine hovers o'er the pile –
> Make this a sacred part of Albion's isle
> (*Don Juan*, XI. xxiv)

George IV's remodelled Carlton House was also to be gaslit so creating an even more glittering southern terminus for Regent Street and 'a fit habitation for an enlightened and powerful prince'.[24] And this aspect of the London streetscape was certainly seen as superior to any European city. This is best encapsulated by Byron who devotes several verses to the street lights:

> The line of lights, too up to Charing Cross,
> Pall Mall, and so forth, have a coruscation
> Like gold as in comparison to dross,
> Match'd with the Continent's illumination.
> Whose cities Night by no means deigns to gloss.
> The French were not yet a lamp-lighting nation,
> And when they grew so – on their new-found lantern,
> Instead of wicks, they made a wicked man turn
> (*Don Juan*, XI. xxvi)

As gas streetlighting spread across the capital, the city by night began to shed its threatening image. The streets became lively evening environments and the magnificent new architecture of the West End glittered in recognition of its new residents. Charles Dickens describes this new illuminated world in *Nicholas Nickleby* (1839):

They rattled on through the noisy, bustling, crowded streets of London, now displaying long double rows of brightly-burning lamps, dotted here and there with the chemists' glaring lights and illuminated besides with the brilliant flood that streamed from the windows of the shops. ... Streams of people apparently without end poured on and on, jostling each other in the crowd and hurrying forward. ... while vehicles of all shapes and makes, mingled up together in one moving mass like running water, lent their ceaseless roar to swell the noise and tumult.

Here, unusually, Dickens also draws attention to the sounds of the metropolis vivifying an otherwise silent spectacle. Perhaps the rarity of descriptions of auditory experiences of the metropolis in early nineteenth-century writings is due in part to the contemporary belief in the unrecordability of sound and the absence of a coherent and effective vocabulary to describe the auditory experience of the metropolis.

Creating a bourgeois urban utopia

In the period 1800–1840 the streets of London were reorientated and the sensory experience of the city became more contrived and self-consciously constructed. As urban experience became planned and shaped rather than a haphazard random side product of disparate building projects, so the debates about urban aesthetics proliferated. Perhaps unsurprisingly as state bureaucracies increased alongside commercial and social systems so rationality and organised space began to predominate so representing this kind of modernity. The first moves towards rationalising the street layout of west London included the construction of Regent Street.[25] The street forged a line north–south through the centre of London and carved through the existing urban plan to redefine access, circulation and vista through the metropolis (Figure 2.4). It was designed to provide an essential link between the new development of Marylebone Park on the northern edge of London and the city centre. The desire to add majesty and grandeur to the urban landscape and a spirit of competition with France were essential components in the evolution and instigation of the Regent Street project.[26]

The New Street, as Regent Street was called until 1820, was to be flanked by impressive terraces of houses, offices and shops. Colonnades fronted some of the terraces to provide shelter from the elements for those shopping at ground level. Above these colonnades were balconies from which the occupants of the dwellings above these commercial premises (usually young single men) could survey the urban scene. The aesthetic considerations for the design of all the Regent Street buildings went beyond the use of classically styled architecture to include colour, as seen in the obligatory use of Bath stone-coloured stucco on all the buildings erected as part of the Regent's Park and Regent Street project.[27] The new street made a considerable intervention in the urban form and altered the experience of the city. Leigh's *New Picture of London* (1820) remarked: '[The] large and capacious street that is now … completed … the effect altogether [with the newly refurbished Carlton House] will be grand, imposing, worthy of a great nation'.[28] The writer goes on to remark that the colonnades of 'the superb row of uniform buildings' which comprise Regent Street are reminiscent of Rome. The

2.4   E. Walker, The Quadrant, Regent Street, 1852. Lithograph

decision made only a few years later to demolish Carlton House and build the Athenaeum and the United Service Clubs on the site did not detract from the importance of Regent Street to the urban aesthetic or infrastructure. This new thoroughfare was laid over the existing urban fabric and represented the rise of the new bourgeois class who experienced the city in a different way. The feeling of opulence and safety was enhanced by the continuous colonnades which flanked the buildings from Oxford Circus to Charing Cross.

Those who have daily intercourse with the public establishments in Westminster, may go 2/3 of the way on foot under cover, and those who have nothing to do but walk about and amuse themselves may do so every day of the week, instead of being frequently confined many days together to their Houses by rain; and such a covered colonnade would be of peculiar convenience to those who require daily exercise. The Balustrades over the Colonnades will form balconies to the lodging rooms over the Shops, from which the occupiers of the lodgings can see and converse with those passing in Carriages underneath, and which will add to the gaiety of the scene, and induce single men, and others, who only visit Town occasionally, to give a preference to such Lodgings.[29]

The emphasis here is not only on the importance of social interaction of persons of appropriate class but also on the anonymous viewing of this social ritual by outsiders or anonymous flâneurs, here referred to as 'the single men ... who only visit Town occasionally', who complete this metropolitan scene. The recognition of these different kinds of social exchange signifies a new kind of urban self-consciousness which helped to shape urban experience and social life in London. This eradication of the previous street plan in the interests of the urban bourgeoisie is akin to de Certeau's notion of the 'Concept City'. Here 'rational organization must repress all the physical, mental and political pollutions that would compromise it'.[30] And it is difficult to find another urban planning project in early nineteenth-century London where the physical (architectural), mental (experiential) or political considerations have been such driving forces. Critics of the Regent Street 'utopia' saw it instead as a threat to public safety and decency. Lord Glenbervie[31] exclaimed that the colonnades – the very symbol of Augustan grandeur – were: 'pretty on paper "but" such a repository for Damp, Obscurity, Filth and Indecency as no regulation or Police will be able to prevent'.[32]

But more important than this material objection is the notion of this rationalised plan as being a dystopia. Indeed de Certeau's own counter-argument presented in the idea of the opaque city reveals that like any text a city can have different readings and meanings. And this 'migrational, or metaphorical, city thus slips into the text of the clear, planned readable city'[33] to challenge the rational, formal abstraction of the 'Enlightenment project'. The irrational objection of the residents of Cavendish Square to the original proposed line of Regent Street signifies how projects concerned with embodying a social caste in the urban plan and policing the new environment were ruptured by the illegible improvisations of those for whom it was designed. They objected in the strongest terms to the new street as it would drastically reduce the amount of land and outbuildings to the rear of their properties. As a consequence the street was rerouted about 100 yards to the east and had to make a sharp turn to the northwest to meet up with Portland Place. Here, the irregularity of the London street plan triumphed over the rational scheme which would have enabled the quick circulation of troops through the city in case of unrest.[34] It must be remembered that the rationalised street plans were new and unfamiliar to contemporary residents and were both threatening and alluring. In this way the city became, as Lefebvre suggests, an intellectual and architectural labyrinth. This mythical quality of London represented its modernity and reproduced the dreamed-of architecture of the ancients: the labyrinth with all its virtual and actual complexities. The new utopian city replaced the old London but the experience of it for residents and visitors retained the imprint of its early modern predecessor.

The most striking bourgeois urban utopia of the opening years of the nineteenth century was Marybone Park or as it became known, the Regent's Park (Figure 2.5).[35] This speculative development, with the Crown as landlord, was to be quite different from the Georgian squares to the

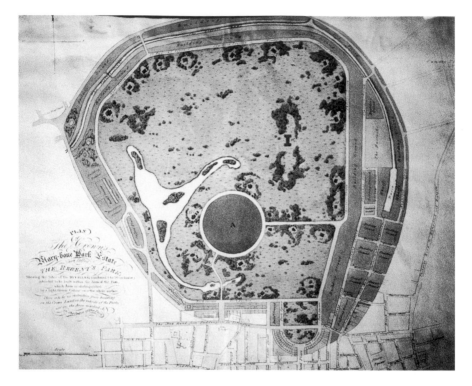

2.5   Plan of the Crown's Mary-le-bone Park Estate, now called The Regent's Park, showing the proposed sites of 26 villas, 1826

south of it. The area was to be encircled by terraces of houses with façades in the mode of grand palaces.[36] The parkland was to be landscaped and 56 villas were to be built in the parkland in such a way as to make each villa appear as if it alone enjoyed all the surrounding landscape. Alongside the villas the park was to contain a church, a new barracks, a royal pavilion and national valhalla. The planning was formal with a series of concentric circuses and perimeter roads.

For the first time a coherent, rational plan was produced as part of this very rapid development of London. The new street was vital to link the new area with central London and especially to the Houses of Parliament. This was recognised as early as 1809 when the surveyor John Fordyce remarked:

Distance is best computed by time; and if means could be found to lessen the time of going from Marybone to the Houses of Parliament, the value of the ground for building would be thereby proportionately increased. The best and probably upon the whole, the most advantageous way of doing that, would be by opening a great street from Charing-Cross towards a central part of Marylebone Park.[37]

The new road from the park to Charing Cross would reduce travelling time by one-third. This plan also introduced focal points into the urban streetscape which helped orientate those travelling through the city and became in turn social and cultural markers.

Focal points

The importance of vistas and focal points in the new urban streetscape was of prime concern as the experience of the metropolis at ground level was the subject of a conscious re-structuring. Many of the ideas were embodied in John Nash's vision of the new modern metropolis. Describing his grand scheme for London Nash stated:

Every length of street would be terminated by a façade of beautiful architecture … and to add to the beauty of approach from Westminster to Charing Cross, a square or crescent, open to and looking down Parliament Street might be built around the Equestrian Statue at Charing Cross which at the same time that it would enlarge that space from whence as before observed the greatest part of the population of the Metropolis meet and diverge, it could afford a magnificent and beautiful termination of the street from Westminster. The lofty situation of Charing Cross and gradual assent to it are peculiarly calculated to produce a grand and striking effect. Such a building might be appropriated to additional offices for the Government or Royal Academy or Antiquarian Society might be placed there.[38]

These ideas were taken up in an Act which received the royal assent on 10 June 1813, 'An act for a more convenient communication from Mary le Bone Park and the Northernmost Parts of the Metropolis … to Charing Cross … and for the making of a more convenient sewage for the same'.[39] This Act also included provision for the 'widening [of] Cockspur Street from the south end of Haymarket to Charing Cross; and forming an open square in the King's Mews opposite Charing Cross'. By 1825 the Commissioners of Woods and Forests wished to develop this area into a square at the junction of Whitehall, St Martin's Lane, the Strand and Pall Mall East and to improve the communications through the west of the metropolis which included the widening of the western end of the Strand. Nash was also asked to devise a

more commodious access from the Houses of Parliament … to the British Museum and the numerous respectably occupied new buildings in the part of the Metropolis, in which that Great National Repository is now being permanently established.[40]

These are significant developments in the history of London's planning. For the first time commodious access to all parts of the city and links between public buildings appear on the agenda. But the dream and reality of the modern metropolis were at variance as many of these schemes remained only part finished or never left the drawing board.[41]

The uniformity of the London terraces of houses gave the streets a domestic rather than a majestic urban aesthetic. The sight made a considerable impression on visitors as one German tourist remarked:

I anticipated great palaces and saw nothing but mere small houses. But their very uniformity and their limitless extent impress the soul wonderfully. These houses of brick, owing to the damp atmosphere and coal smoke, are all of a uniform colour, that is to say of a brown olive green … while the broad and accurately squared streets which these houses form, seem to be bordered by endlessly long barracks.[42]

The vastness of London was emphasised by the long uniform streets which according to de Quincey offered 'the continual opening of transient glimpses into other vistas equally far stretching … aiding that sense of vastness and illimitable proportions which for ever brood over the aspect of London in its interior'.[43]

The garden squares greatly enhanced the cityscape providing punctuation points in the network of streets and places to encounter other residents and walkers. Leigh's *New Picture of London* (1820) remarked:

The Promenades about the metropolis besides those included in the Royal parks, Kensington Gardens, &c are so numerous … Temple and Gray's Inn Gardens and some families have exclusive use of elegant walks and grounds in some fashionable squares in which they reside.[44]

Certainly Russell Square was frequently mentioned in guidebooks to London. *The Ambulator* (1811) described Russell Square as 'remarkable for the elegance of its houses, its ornamental area and the very fine bronze statue of the late Duke of Bedford'.[45] Bloomsbury was sometimes commented upon. *The Picture of London* (1815) describes Bloomsbury beginning with Russell Square thus:

Russell Square on a side of Bloomsbury is one of the largest and finest squares in London. Broad streets intersect it at the corner and middle which add to its beauty and remove general objection to squares by ventilating the air … the extensive enclosure is a square containing oval shrubberies, a square lawn in the centre intersected with gravel walks.[46]

This recognition of the contribution Bloomsbury made to the metropolis is followed by the eager anticipation of the construction of Regent Street and its 'ornamental' effect on London.

These punctuation points were essentially domestic. The grand vision for Regent Street promised some relief from the monotony of the London terraces and offered a new social environment. But how were these different environments combined to re-image London into the nation's capital?

Notes

1. J. Britton, *A Brief Account of the Colosseum*, London, 1829, 3.

2. The idea of the flâneur was first postulated in the early nineteenth century by Balzac and taken up by Charles Baudelaire in his *Painter of Modern Life* (*Peintre de la Vie Moderne*) (1859–60). Walter Benjamin's essay on Baudelaire written in the 1930s provides an interesting critique on Baudelaire ideas about modernity and the role of the flâneur in the modern city. See Walter Benjamin, *Charles Baudelaire, a Lyric Poet on the Eve of High Capitalism*, trans. H. Zohn, London, Verso, 1983. This way of viewing urban space is discussed in S. Buck-Morss, *Dialectics of Seeing: Walter Benjamin and the arcades project*, Cambridge, Mass., MIT, 1986.

3. The privileging of vision over other senses has constructed a way of seeing which is predominantly male. In this context sight, vision or views of the metropolis can present a skewed analysis of the experience of the city by men and women. This issue is fully discussed by Doreen Massey, 'Flexible Sexism', *Society and Space*, 9(1), 1991, 45 esp.

4. W. Benjamin, 'Paris – Capital of the Nineteenth Century', *Reflections*, trans. E. Jephcott, New York, Harcourt, Brace and Jovanovich, 1979, 150.

5. Letter from T. Moore to J. Corry, 24 October 1811 as quoted in J. Summerson, *John Nash Architect to King George IV*, London, 1949, 107.

6. See D. Arnold, 'Paris Haussman: Le Pari d'Haussman', *The Architects' Journal*, 1991.

7. J. B. B. Barjaud and C. P. Landon, *Description de Londres et de ses environs*, Paris, 1810.

8. William Darton, *A Description of London: a sketch of the history and present state and almost all celebrated public buildings*, London, 1824.

9. See chapter 1, p. 10.

10. Daniel Defoe, *The Fortunes and Misfortunes of the Famous Moll Flanders*, London, 1722.

11. S. E. Rasmussen, *London the Unique City*, Cambridge, Mass., MIT, 1982, 198–200.

12. *The Picture of London*, 1802, 66.

13. Pattens were shoes made thick or set in an iron ring to raise the wearer's feet out of the mud.

14. *Picture of London*, 1802, 268.

15. Thomas de Quincey, *The Nation of London*, 1834, 182.

16. See Walter Benjamin, 'Central Park', *New German Critique*, 34, Winter, 1985.

17. See H. Lefebvre, *The Production of Space*, Oxford, Basil Blackwell, 1991.

18. See M. de Certeau, *The Practice of Everyday Life*, Berkeley, University of California Press, 1984.

19. Pierce Egan's *Life in London: the Day and Night Scenes of Jerry Hawthorn Esq. and his elegant friend Corinthian Tom, accompanied by Bob Logic, the Oxonian, in their Rambles and Sprees through the Metropolis*, 1821, 343.

20. J. B. B. Barjaud and C. P. Landon *op. cit.*

21. *The Ambulator*, 1811, 23.

22. John Evelyn, *Fumifugium*, 1661.

23. Byron probably wrote Canto XI of his epic poem *Don Juan* in 1822–3. Juan is visiting London shortly after the end of the second Russian–Turkish War in 1791. The anachronistic description of the effect of the London street lights is a testament to their striking presence in the city.

24. Leigh's *New Picture of London*, London, 1820, 218.

25. This name was not given to the street until 1820. Up until this time it was referred to as the New Street. Both names are used in this chapter.

26. Sir John Summerson, *The Life and Work of John Nash, Architect*, London, 1980, chs 6 and 10 and T. Davis, *John Nash: The Prince Regent's Architect*, London, 1966, ch. 5.

27. This is mentioned in a lease taken out by James Burton on a plot of land in Regent's Park, Cres 6/131 f 47. The conditions laid down by Nash were typical for those of the whole Regent's Park and Regent Street project.

28. Leigh's *New Picture of London*, London, 1820, 218.

29.   *First Report*, 1812, 89.

30.   M. de Certeau *op. cit.*, ch. 7, part III 'Walking the City', 91–110. Here the concern is with the urban reformers but the principles of eradication, renewal and the creation of 'un espace propre' hold true in the development of London at this time.

31.   Sylvester Douglas, Lord Glenbervie was a fellow civil servant of John Fordyce. Conflicting accounts of his abilities and commitment to the Metropolitan Improvements appear in A. Saunders, *Regent's Park from 1086 to the present day*, London, Bedford College, 1981 and J. Mordaunt Crook, 'Metropolitan Improvements: John Nash and the Picturesque', in C. Fox (ed.), *London World City 1800–1840*, Yale, New Haven and London, 1992, 77–96.

32.   PRO Cres 26/17.

33.   M. de Certeau *op. cit.*, 'Walking the City', 93.

34.   For a full discussion of this aspect of London's urban plan see D. Arnold, 'Rationality, Safety and Power: the street planning of later Georgian London', *The Georgian Group Journal*, 1995, 37–50. These ideas about urban planning were influential in Baron Haussman's remodelling of Paris later in the century. For a discussion of this see D. Arnold, 'Paris Haussman: Le Pari d'Haussman', *Architects' Journal*, 1991.

35.   For a full discussion of the building of the villas in the Regent's Park see D. Arnold, 'A Family Affair: James and Decimus Burton's work in the Regent's Park' in D. Arnold (ed.) *The Georgian Villa*, Stroud and New York, Sutton Publishing, 1998, 105–17.

36.   Nash drew his inspiration from France especially the façades of the Louvre and Versailles.

37.   The Surveyor General's Triennial Report no. 4, 1809.

38.   1812 Report, 90.

39.   53 Geo. III, c. 121.

40.   Fifth Report to His Majesties Commissioners of Woods Forests and Land Revenues, London, 1826.

41.   For a useful survey of some of the more ambitious schemes for London at this time see F. Barker and R. Hyde, *London as it Might Have Been*, London, John Murray, 1982.

42.   Heinrich Heine, *English Fragments*, 1828.

43.   Thomas de Quincey, *The Nation of London*, 1834.

44.   Leigh's *New Picture of London*, London, 1820, 225.

45.   *The Ambulator*, London, 1811, 23.

46.   *The Picture of London*, 3rd edn, London, 1815, 159–60.

3

The Nation of London

The re-imaging of London in the opening decades of the nineteenth century had a considerable impact on the architecture and experience of the city for both resident and visitor alike. The ideology behind the transformation of the metropolis from a domestic-scale capital to first city of Empire – in particular the idea of nationhood and nationalism – presents London as a self-consciously constructed artefact or text. The interaction of the social, political and economic readings of the city produces the idea of the nation of London which had currency in the writings about the metropolis. In the years 1800–1840, in the wake of the Act of Union of 1798, a new national identity began to emerge which was centred around several elements including the celebration of the final defeat of the French and the re-enforcing of the political position of the Hanoverian monarchy. The impact on the culture and society of early nineteenth-century Britain was considerable and found particular focus in the capital city. London continued to increase in geographical size, in population and in political and economic importance to such an extent that it was seen to represent the nation. The aesthetic consequences of this in terms of architecture and urban planning – can be seen in the Metropolitan Improvements which proposed wide-ranging developments and changes intended to make the city more physically beautiful. The metropolis played an important part in the promotion of a common national persona and urban beauty was used as a tool to instil a sense of pride and social responsibility in the populace. Moreover, the heroes who had defeated the French were represented in the new urban landscape in the form of freestanding monuments and architectural sculpture. This helped to develop a distinct iconographic scheme and urban narrative and refine the experience of the urban aesthetic. In this way the architecture, planning and narratives of the city were harnessed in the service of the state to promote a feeling of unity, well-being and nationhood. This new metropolitan identity was underpinned by funda-mental changes in the social and governmental systems and their mutual interaction. Not least the increasing number of middle-class residents both necessitated and facilitated bureaucratic processes. Many of these were self-referential and served to consolidate information – for instance the census begun in 1801. But the common focus of these processes was to ensure a unified communality across all classes under the umbrella of one nation. London, as a centre of these new systems and the most impressive city in Britain, represented these complex and intertwined elements of the modern state. The nation of London was a bourgeois utopia which re-presented the increasing state bureaucracy and new social systems of the modern metropolis. But what was the relationship between nationalism and the modernity of the metropolis?

Nationalism – the codification of a set of political and social values into an identifiable force – can be seen as both an abstract concept and a construct of the state and/or monarch.[1] It stands distinct from the nation state which has its roots in Lockean philosophy where the individual begins to assert his/her own importance and identity in affairs of state. This implies that an individual identifies with the processes and mechanisms of the state rather than being loyal to one nation. The state is a concrete, identifiable body with political interests and recognisable procedural apparatus. The nation and the concept of nationalism is more speculative. It is a tool to focus loyalty and this is achieved through the promotion of the idea of nation as a community of descent without ethnic restraints which has a degree of self-conscious-ness, which implies a nation should be self-defined. This definition, however, also encompasses the doctrine of popular freedom and sovereignty where the people (*sic* nation) are liberated from external constraint. This necessi-tates a single public culture – the creation of an authentic identity. In this way the concept of nationalism which developed in the opening years of the nineteenth century can be summarized as being made up of autonomy, unity and identity.[2] This enables an alignment of individuals across classes along social, economic and political lines around a central focus or leading group. In the case of the early nineteenth century this focus was the state and the monarch as both the titular head of state and symbolic embodiment of the nation. The importance of this self-conscious re-imaging and renewal of London for both the present and the future was recognised by contemporary commentators:

The 'apperelling of the state' is an affair of more importance than it appears at first view. Our descendants and foreigners will probably view the structures we raise, for five hundred years, and they will in some degree determine the character of the country and of the period.[3]

This idea of Britishness had already found expression in John Flaxman's unrealised plan in 1799 for a 230 ft statue of Britannia – Divine providence triumphant – to celebrate the Battle of the Nile. It represented both a triumphant nation and the genius of the Empire. On its imposing site on Greenwich Hill it would have dominated the metropolis. Flaxman recognised the potential of this colossus in the construction of an urban nationalistic iconography as he remarked 'it is a work intended to last as long as the Trajan Column, the Amphitheatre and the Pyraminds of Egypt'.

Making the nation

Marxist historians, most notably here, Eric Hobsbawm, identify nationalism as necessary in the creation of a national market economy and a viable national bourgeois class. Here nation, nationalism, the nation state, national symbols and histories are all presented as part of an invented tradition.[4] Hobsbawn positions his discussion in relationship to mid to late nineteenth-century France. Here the standardisation of administration and law are presented as elements which transform the people into citizens of a specific country. The invention of public ceremonies is an important part of this, for instance Bastille day instituted in 1880. The mass production of public monuments and developments in urban planning are also important elements in the invention of this nationalistic tradition. Hobsbawn's model, which fits well into his underlying materialist thesis, is one of an industrialised bourgeois society. Can such an interpretation be used to explain the re-imaging of early nineteenth-century London and the experience of this self-consciously produced public culture? There are, without doubt, some common phenomena which are part of the continuing dialogue between the two capital cities. But in the case of London the essential ingredient for the establishment of a bourgeois culture through nationalism is the important relationship between state and monarch in the promotion of a nationalist culture. This impacts on the bourgeois experience of the metropolis as seen in the new urban plans, the development of the urban picturesque and conscious changes made by the state/monarch and speculative developers to the demographic make-up of London. The aesthetic development of London at this time is a manifestation of these underlying, nationalistic cultural ideals which resulted in the codification of society and social rituals through academies and education and imposed a shared culture on a previously existing complex structure of localised groups. The public 'body politic' was an essential part of this identity as Hazlitt remarked:

We have a sort of abstract existence; and a community of ideas and knowledge (rather than local proximity) is the bond of society and good fellowship. This is the one great cause of the tone of political feeling in large and populous cities. There is here a visible body-politic, a type and image of that huge Leviathan the State. We comprehend that vast denomination, the *People*, of which we see a tenth part daily moving before us; and by having our imaginations emancipated from petty interests and personal dependence, we learn to venerate ourselves as men, and to respect the rights of human nature. Therefore it is that the citizens and freemen of London and Westminster are patriots by prescription, philosophers and politicians by the right of their birthplace.[5]

The city was then an essential location for this new national identity. The concept of London as a complete entity with an improved aesthetic, infrastructure and a greater sense of connectedness in the urban plan represented these nationalistic ideals and a new, coherent social structure.

The re-imaging of London can also be seen as a reaction against something – in this case the French. The French wars had left deep political and economic scars on the cultural landscape of Britain. This reaction was a manifestation of a fundamental re-evaluation of the make-up of British society that occurred at the end of the eighteenth century. Up until the American War of Independence and the French Revolution, Britain was seen as a liberal, democratic country. But these two events shook up this idea and re-defined Britain's place on the political map. Compared with the egalitarianism of America and France, Britain no longer seemed the bastion of liberalism. The political implications of this change in the perception of Britain are not the subject here. However, the change in perception does impinge on a fundamental question relevant to the work in London: the influence of Parisian models. The prolonged period of animosity with France might have left Britain predisposed to reject the developments in architecture and urban planning instigated by Napoleon I in Paris. But this would have meant ignoring the language of triumphalism encoded in design elements such as arches, columns and squares (fora) which had their roots in ancient Rome. Moreover, if the idea of nation can be achieved through the mass production of monuments and urban planning it is important to choose a symbolism which is easily recognised and has an established iconography. The feeling of competition between the two capitals went beyond urban planning and monuments to encompass cultural ideals. Frequent mention was made in the Parliamentary Reports of Parisian urban planning, especially the rue du Rivoli. But beyond this the development of the British Museum in terms of its collections and architecture was intended to challenge the Louvre, which was viewed as a rival ahead in the cultural race.[6] But the rationale behind these monuments was seen as distinctive to their French counterparts which were '[raised] merely as a triumph to national vanity'.[7]

The achievements of the French provided a concept of otherness essential for the development of British nationalism and a benchmark for cultural progress which needed to be superseded. Waterloo, where the French were finally defeated, had a unifying effect on the nation and provided obvious choices for national symbols of victory: monuments and the autonomous hero. A committee known as the 'Committee of Taste' had been set up in 1802 to oversee the expenditure upon monuments to the British war dead from funds voted by parliament. Its membership included Richard Payne Knight, Sir George Beaumont and the Marquis of Stafford. The fusion of victory, nationalism and the Metropolitan Improvements is seen in the committee's call in 1816 to members of the Royal Academy to produce designs for a 'National Monument'.[8]

The monuments and urban planning of a triumphant London helped to define British nationalism by celebrating the defeat of the French and representing a new British identity. The architectural vocabulary and syntax used to construct the message of the buildings and monuments were common to French and British architects as they studied the same antique sources and there was a significant international exchange of ideas about urban planning and design. But British architects used this triumphalistic language to articulate a different narrative to that of their French counterparts. The story told by the re-imaging of London in the period 1800–1840 had a far more wide-ranging scope than simply victory over the French and included the celebration of the intellectual achievements of Britain and the strengths of indigenous British culture. This combination of meanings is not new in itself but in the opening years of the nineteenth century it took on a new dimension particularly in the face of the changing social make-up of the populace.

Linda Colley argues that a national British identity was forged in the eighteenth century.[9] It was needed whilst Britain was under threat from France and was defined principally as being a contrast to the otherness of France. Colley argues that this notion of Britishness codified the idea of freedom as being commensurate with class structure and states 'crudely, but fundamentally, class and nation in Britain at this time were not antithetical but two sides of the same historical process'. In other words class consciousness was part of a developing national consciousness. Towards the close of the eighteenth century this need for faith in a superior identity was heightened by the threat from France. This identity was personified in figures like John Bull and the emergence of the new cultural phenomena of home tourism and introduced the idea of the picturesque into the reading of the landscape of Britain. This gave a solid, tangible identity to superior Britishness. The American War of Independence and the French Revolution redefined Britain's political image and challenged its position as the bastion of liberty and democracy. But elements of this national identity did survive into the opening years of the nineteenth century and influenced the development of the urban plan of London.

Housing the nation

One of the key strands of this new national identity to survive into the early nineteenth century was the continuing development of a class consciousness as part of an evolving national consciousness. This had already been encoded into the most fundamental component of the city: the townhouse. The 1774 Building Acts established four different rates of houses by size and grade of materials.[10] Commensurate with this was the association of the different rates of houses with various classes of occupants; first-rate houses commanded higher rents than those of a lower rating. This made zoning possible as the building of houses of a certain rate would, in theory, ensure a certain class of occupier. In this way the decisions made by landlord and builder had a distinct impact on the demography of an area and patterns of population and class across London. The Acts did, in effect, enable the identification of housing stock for different social classes. This identification is not foolproof – larger houses could provide lodgings for several families and the desirability of areas could change. But the rate system did facilitate the creation of areas with distinctive social aspirations. Late eighteenth- and early nineteenth-century Bloomsbury is an interesting case study in this context (Figure 3.1). Much of the building work was carried out during a time when the relationship of the area to the centre of London was going through changes – the area was now to the east of the centre but had the benefit of the New Road, begun in the 1750s, which ran east–west along the northern edge of London.

Bloomsbury was mostly constructed by the very successful speculative developer James Burton. Between 1792 and 1814 Burton built 1756 houses in the area (Tables 3.1 and 3.2). Developers had a considerable impact on the demography of an area for although landowners sometimes specified that houses should be of either first or second rate, the final decision lay with the builder.[11] Houses of lower rates were often placed on the edges of developments to provide accommodation for the necessary merchants and servants. Sometimes these were additional to the original development agreement and enhanced the speculator's profits. Indeed, Burton's efforts in Bloomsbury had a striking effect on the London cityscape. Certainly Russell Square, one of the area's finest, was frequently mentioned in guidebooks to London. Burton's designs for uniform terraces of houses ranged around crescents and squares which provided agreeable open space made Bloomsbury a distinctive area of the city. This was often commented on by guidebooks and writers on London. *The Picture of London*'s description of Bloomsbury begins with Russell Square where the landscape gardener Humphry Repton had been employed by Burton to lay out the grounds.[12]

The unified façades of the West End terraces and the introduction of vistas and a more coherent urban plan across the different estates was another way

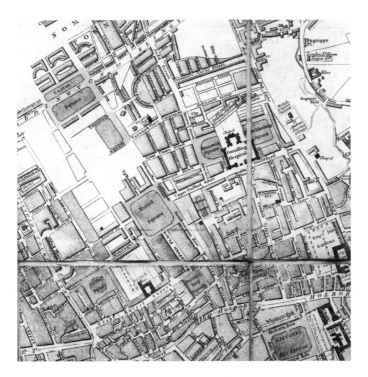

3.1   Detail of map showing plan of Bloomsbury, 1812

of codifying the urban landscape and expressing national identity. The *Picture of London* recognised the importance of garden squares to the image of the metropolis and included a new section devoted to them in the 1815 edition (Figure 3.2). The commentary covered a large number of the London squares of which Grosvenor was seen as the finest with its equestrian statue of George II in the centre and the houses ranged around it were 'some of the most magnificent in the metropolis'. Next in terms of their beauty were Portman, Montague and Manchester squares the latter having 'a small house on the north side [Hertford House] which is one of the best in London'.[13] These features helped to create a kind of upper- and middle-class identity through differentiations in housing rate, street width and landscape which helped these classes to connect with the city. Here again the interaction between social class and the re-shaping of the metropolis presented a unified national image. Moreover, the names of the squares and streets were a reminder of who owned London as Percy's *History* remarked: 'The names and titles of the country residences of our nobility are often perpetuated in our squares and streets, particularly those of the dukes of Bedford, Portland and Grafton.'[14] This language of the city reinforced the class structure which

Table 3.1 Townhouses of all rates constructed by James Burton, 1785–1823

Estate and date of construction	First-rate houses	Second-rate houses	Third-rate houses	Fourth-rate houses	Total	Estimated rental including ground rent (£)	Estimated gross value (£)
Stanford, Bennett and Brunswick Street, Albion Street, Newgate and Giltspur Streets, Eastcheap, Tyndale Place, Crescent Place, New Bridge Street, Water Lane, Old Broad Street, and Clapham Common. 1785–92	17	24	15	14	70	7,420	90,300
Foundling Estate 1792–1802	29	159	172	226	586	36,240	296,700
Bedford Estate 1798–1803	132	43	8	153	336	32,240	299,400
Skinners Estate 1807–16	4	146	284	189	623	21,190	309,600
Lucas Estate 1808–14	1	0	143	67	211	10,120	78,800
Kent 1803–07	3	0	4	20	27	1,500	25,000
Regent Street etc. 1815–23	39	104	38	10	191	29,170	338,400
Regent's Park 1815–23	76	21	14	78	189	25,060	317,100
Colonel Eyre's Estate 1818–23	10	3	116	4	133	9,060	93,600
Totals					2,366	172,000	1,848,900

Source: R. Dobie, *The History of the United Parishes of St Giles in the Field and St George Bloomsbury*, London, 1829; 'Abstract Statement of Buildings erected by or for a Individual, from 1785 to 1823, both inclusive; exclusively of Buildings erected for others under his superintendence'

Table 3.2   James Burton's building activities in Bloomsbury

Estate and date of construction	First-rate houses	Second-rate houses	Third-rate houses	Fourth-rate houses	Total number of houses
Foundling Estate 1792–1802	29	159	172	226	586
Bedford Estate 1798–1803	132	43	8	153	336
Skinners Company Estate 1807–16	4	146	284	189	623
Lucas Estate 1808–14	1	0	143	67	211
Total number of houses	166	348	607	635	1,756

Source: Based on the figures in Table 3.1

3.2   Russell Square and statue of the Duke of Bedford, 1829. Engraving

underpinned the concept of national identity. And the impressive nature of the architecture and urban planning was meant to engender a feeling of national pride. This pattern of development of grand façades and first- and second-rate housing continued in the Regent Street project which was a conscious attempt to zone the city according to class.[15]

National landscapes

Despite the increasing importance of the metropolis in the social and cultural map of Britain in the opening years of the nineteenth century, the
importance of landscape was not forgotten. Home tourism had helped to
develop nationalistic sentiment in the enjoyment of the British landscape.
This was encouraged by writers like Revd William Gilpin who, in the 1780s,
presented templates or guides to tourists on how to interpret views along
picturesque lines evocative of freedom and nationhood. Gilpin's way of
seeing remained influential and prepared the way for the reading of the
urban parks as a complex narrative where the correlation of freedom and
nature inherent in the iconography of English garden design as well as the
landscape was brought into the city for political and nationalistic ends. The
urban landscape became an important element in the creation of nationalist
feeling and a sense of belonging especially for the urban middle class.

The eighteenth-century country house and its garden were symbols of
the new society – aristocratic, leisured, landed and rich. But in the nineteenth century the city became increasingly important and money was
generated by industry, creating a new and significant middle class. But the
powerful influence of the landscape still had resonance in the nineteenth-
century metropolis. Towards the end of the eighteenth century the wars in
Europe and the consequent difficulties for foreign travel had encouraged
home tourism.[16] This activity had developed to include the appreciation of
the landscape in general rather than just landscape gardens, and here
advice was on hand as to how to view it.[17] The political significance of the
landscape and its ability to engender a sense of nationalism, pleasure and/
or well-being in the visitor did not go unnoticed by theorists and Enlightenment thinkers. These principles were used in the urban plan of London
to influence the subjective response of the individual to the new urban
landscape. The theorists had established the symbolic function of landscape and architecture and here it was used in the service of monarch, state
and nation instead of an individual landowner. The educated population
was already accustomed to reading the landscape and it could have dis-
tinctly political associations. In his *Essays on the Picturesque* (1794) Uvedale
Price represents these views as he aligns good government with natural-
ism in landscape:

A good landscape is that in which all the parts are free and unconstrained, but in
which, though some are prominent and highly illuminated, and others in shade and
retirement; some rough, and others more smooth and polished, yet they are all
necessary to the beauty, energy, effect and harmony of the whole. I do not see how
good government can be more exactly defined.[18]

His sentiments were echoed by Humphry Repton who was involved with the landscaping of London especially St James's Park and Russell Square:

I cannot help seeing great affinity betwixt deducing gardening from the painter's studies of nature, and deducing government from the opinions of man in a savage state. The neatness, simplicity, and elegance of English gardening, have acquired the approbation of the present century, as the happy medium betwixt the wildness of nature and the stiffness of art; in the same manner as the English constitution is the happy medium betwixt the liberty of savages, and the restraint of despotic government.[19]

The implications of these attitudes for the reading of urban landscapes come to the fore in the re-development of the Regent's Park and the Royal Parks. The direct association between landscape, politics and a sense of national identity was intensified by the metropolitan context of the Royal Parks. Here the laying out of the landscape using picturesque principles with an emphasis on axiality and vista linking key monuments to national greatness – centring on the Hanoverian dynasty and the nation's heroes – created a new and important urban experience for both the upper and middle classes. There was initial resistance to the artificial imposition of 'landscape' on these urban fields. But as the city continued to increase in size these new environments, now termed *rus in urbe*, became a recognised part of urban experience and social life (Figure 3.3). A contemporary commentator offered this reading of the new urban environment:

A noble Park is rapidly rising up ... laid out with groves, lakes and villas, with their separate pleasure-grounds, while through the whole there is a winding road, which commands at every turn some fresh feature of an extensive country prospect. ... The plan and size of the Park is in every respect worthy of the nation. It is larger than Hyde Park, St James's and Green Park together [and the author] cannot recommend a better thing ... than a day spent wandering amidst the union of stately objects and rural beauty which constitute the charm of Marylebone Park.[20]

George IV received some of the credit for these improvements and their effect on re-imaging of urban experience:

Such are a few of the improvements which have taken place under the auspices of George IV, and if it cannot be said of his majesty, as of the Roman emperor, that he found a city of brick and left one of marble, it cannot be denied that, while he has sustained the national honour abroad, he has done more to patronize literature, to advance fine arts, and to improve the metropolis, than any sovereign that ever wielded the British sceptre, and should providence spare his majesty to complete his designs, and preserve the peace in Europe, we may anticipate that England will continue to be the 1st country and London the first city of the world.[21]

The Augustan theme, based on the re-use of antique Roman architecture and planning ideas, was a popular referent for the monarch and the re-imaging of London: 'As the Augustus of his age, under whose royal auspices the

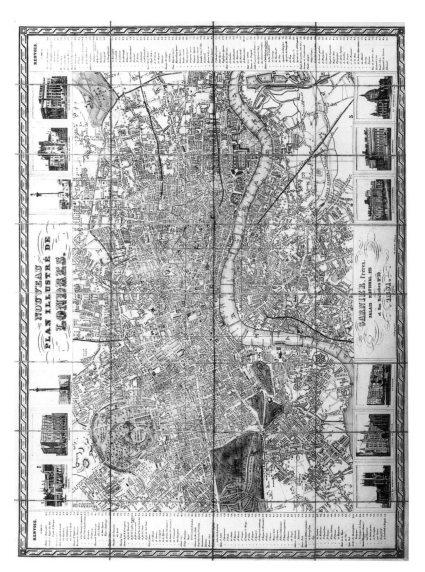

3.3 Garnier, map showing The Regent's Park, Hyde Park, St James's Park and Green Park, 1851

Metropolis of Britain has received embellishments of such magnitude as to become the admiration of all the world'.[22]

The parks were also the site of events staged to embellish the popularity and status of the monarchy such as the National Jubilee in 1814 to celebrate a century of the Hanoverian dynasty.[23] The public's access to royal land was seen as a great bonus for city dwellers. Percy's *History* remarked 'It is fortunate for the inhabitants of London that the parks are royal "demesnes" as they were, not least, the lungs of the metropolis'.[24] The overall benefits for the population and the general feeling of well-being were seen to be such that concern was expressed that although the western half of London was well endowed with the public open spaces the north and east had very few. These feelings found official voice in the Committee on Public Walks 1833 which called for more land owned by the Crown and the Duchy of Cornwall in these areas to be turned over for public use. It also summarized the aims and achievements of the development of the Royal Parks and their status within the urban fabric:

St James's Park, Green Park and Hyde Park ... afford to the inhabitants of this Western portion of the Metropolis inestimable advantages as Public Walks. The two latter Parks are open to all classes. St James's Park has lately been planted and improved with great taste, and the interior is now opened, as well [as] Kensington gardens, to all persons well-behaved and properly dressed. Your Committee remark with pleasure the advantage they afford to the Public, as also the great facility of approach to this beautiful Park, caused by opening a handsome stone footway from the bottom of Regent-street: for this accommodation it is understood the Public are indebted to His present Majesty.[25]

The public gaze was to be directed to symbols of the nation which stood both inside and outside the parks. The combined experience of 'common ownership' of these public open spaces and a coherent national identity gave Londoners a sense of belonging.

The national hero

During and immediately after the Napoleonic wars London became a site/ sight of celebration of victories over and of the eventual defeat of the French. As a physical site of sights of celebration the metropolis functioned as a signifier of a distinctive national consciousness and in turn this consciousness shaped the city itself. The projected improvements were numerous and included

new palaces for the sovereign and the Duke of Wellington – a national monument as memorial of our naval victories, another to the memory of general, officers and soldiers, a new custom house, Post Office and several bridges.[26]

3.4   Sir John Soane, RA, design for Hyde Park and St James's Park Entrance, n.d. Watercolour over graphite on three joined sheets of wove paper

All of which underscored the role of the metropolis as a nexus of nationalistic sensibilities.[27] The importance of the urban landscape was not forgotten here as the Royal Parks were the site for many of the plans for these new palaces. Sir John Soane proposed a vast new residence for George IV in Hyde Park together with a new entrance to London and Hyde Park Corner (Figure 3.4), and of the many designs for a metropolitan Waterloo Palace, Joseph Michael Gandy's of 1816 placed the grand residence appropriately in the Regent's Park.[28]

The Augustan image of London was a potent theme in the new urban landscape. George IV, perhaps taking his lead from Napoleon, used the opportunities of the victories at Trafalgar and Waterloo to bolster his own position as they afforded ample opportunity for celebration. One of the principal elements in this self-consciously constructed environment was the triumphal arch. Parisian examples provided useful models: the ceremonial Arch du Triumph for the Arch at Constitution Hill and Charles Percier and Pierre Fontaine's Arc du Carrousel (1806–10) and the Marble Arch formed part of the entrance to the Tuileries Palace and Buckingham Palace respectively.

Monuments to the nation's military prowess played an equally important part in the assertion of the power of the state and there were many proposals for commemorative archways, columns and even mausolea to Nelson and Wellington to be placed at strategic points across the city.[29] George IV also harnessed the nation's enthusiasm for these into his own service and, usefully, a fund of £300,000 had been voted by parliament in 1816 to fund these projects. The Marble Arch and the Arch at Constitution Hill were to be decorated with sculptural celebrations of Britain's military victories, intellectual prowess and the Hanoverian dynasty themes which were also common to the sculptural decoration of the façade of Buckingham Palace.[30] A plaster model of the Marble Arch shows that an equestrian statue of George IV was to surmount the attic in front of which was to be a free-standing group of Wellington and his aides. The subjects of the frieze and decorative sculptural panels in low and high relief narrated the Battle of Waterloo, the life of Nelson and the figure of Fame displaying Britain's military and naval victories. There was also a royal presence in the form of two reliefs showing the king's approbation of the plans before the Battle of Waterloo and the king rewarding Wellington after the battle (Figure 3.5).[31] A similar iconographic message was to be displayed in the sculptural decoration of the Arch at Constitution Hill and at Buckingham Palace, so drawing together the whole composition of palace and monumental entrance ways.[32] These were designed to evoke nationalist feeling through the celebration of victory over the French and British cultural achievements. But here the achievements of the Duke of Wellington and Lord Admiral Nelson formed part of a larger

3.5   John Nash, Marble Arch, 1825–30

narrative. In the context of the evolution of national symbols Wellington and Nelson were regarded not only as men who had achieved military and naval victories over France but also as secular saints who symbolised national virtues. The self-sacrifice of Nelson was annexed by the state to augment the power of these monuments. But the depiction of 'Lord Wellington' was more problematic. One area of debate amongst the designers, including Flaxman, Westmacott and others, was the drapery of Wellington and Nelson.[33] As Nelson had done the decent thing and died he could easily be depicted in classical flowing robes, but what of Wellington? The use of an antique formula in the Achilles Statue (1822) in Hyde Park, which had been commissioned and paid for by a committee of women, had already caused a stir (Figure 3.6). Here Wellington was represented as a victorious athlete but this living hero was shown nude and this ran counter to the modern nation he continued to represent. Wellington was still commander in chief of the British army and a politician, so surely full military dress was necessary for any depiction of him in the sculptural decoration of a new palace and its triumphal arches. But this 'living' image did not correspond to the associations with antiquity, ancient virtue and self-sacrifice which formed an important part of the iconographic message of the whole.

3.6   George Cruikshank, Making Decent – !! – A hint to the Society for the Suppression of Vice, 1822. Coloured etching

Heroic spaces

The notion of sacrifice, and within this heroism, plays a fundamental role in the development of urban planning in London and was a key strand in the developing urban iconography which reflected nationhood, imperialistic triumphalism and, in contradiction, the ever-encroaching metropolitan, bourgeois system of government. The attempts to commemorate the Duke of Wellington and Lord Admiral Nelson for their respective victories at Waterloo and Trafalgar reveal differing aspects of the role of the hero in the construction of a unifying national identity.[34] This shows how national heroes were commodified by the bourgeois culture they were used to represent. The physical construction of the notion of heroism is particularly important in capitalistic consumer-driven societies. This is traced back, in anthropological terms, by Georges Bataille who identifies a truly militaristic society as a venture society from which war is a means of development of power, an orderly progression of Empire.[35] In terms of architecture and urban planning this has led to the production of different kinds of signifier of these concepts. Street names were one way in which the city could become a site of commemoration for heroes. The nomenclature helped shape urban experience and served as a reminder to both civic and national virtue. Percy's *History* identified 18 places named after Nelson, 11 after Trafalgar, 14 after Wellington and 10 sites named after Waterloo. Perhaps the most important additions to the urban fabric in this context were monuments and mausolea to individual greatness – particularly the nation's heroes Wellington and Nelson. The nationalistic qualities of these structures is summed up early in the period by William Wood in his 'Essay on National and Sepulchral Monuments' of 1808. He wrote of the need to build monuments to commemorate great national heroes and enthusiastically endorsed mausolea as a means of doing this:

from the most remote antiquity, until the present moment, from savages of the southern hemisphere, to the polished nations of Europe, all mankind have agreed in erecting sepulchral monuments, to mark their admiration of the illustrious dead.

Attempts to acknowledge the Duke of Wellington's military achievement at Waterloo included the planned gift of a Waterloo Palace equal in grandeur to Blenheim which had been awarded the Duke of Marlborough on his greatest victory. This like many of the planned sculptural monuments to the Duke was not realised, although Wellington did eventually find a London residence in Apsley House which he purchased from his brother in 1829. But the metropolis bore the imprint of this national hero in other ways. Not least the Strand Bridge was renamed Waterloo Bridge.[36] The plain doric form of Waterloo Bridge was appropriately plain and masculine and it was considered one of the sights of the modern metropolis. Percy's *History* went so far as to describe it as 'a work not less pre-eminent amongst the bridges of all ages and countries than the event which it will commemorate as it is unravelled in the annals of ancient or modern history'.[37] But the most apposite commodification of the Duke of Wellington as a national hero is found in the first portion of the New Street to be built: Waterloo Place (1815–16). The Place was the ultimate speculative development. It combined the elements of capitalistic risk and gain which were essential for a bourgeois culture and the hierarchical social system now embodied in the classification of town houses which endorsed the status quo and the identity of the nation. It comprised private houses, the façades of which were decorated with the orders not unlike the Place Vendôme. At the southern end of the square was the screen of Carlton House – a royal residence. The up-market houses flanked the east and west sides of the square and its north end was open to the beginning of Regent Street, the hub of bourgeois urban activity.

A national church

Britain was the only country in Europe with a national church – the Church of England. At its head was the monarch. The 25 years of intermittent warfare which preceded the Battle of Waterloo saw little in the way of church building but the city had continued to grow through the almost indefatigable efforts of speculative developers. This resulted in an imbalance between the demography of London and the location of its churches. The growing concerns about national moral and religious standards were frequently voiced, particularly by the politically impotent middle class. But the founding of the Church Building Society in 1818 prompted action and the Church Building Act came in the same year. The Commissioners received a grant of £1,000,000, superseding the £300,000 voted by parliament in 1816 for the celebration of national heroes, which remained largely unspent. Thirty-eight churches had been built by 1828 and were known as the Waterloo Churches as, their apologists claimed, they were meant to celebrate the defeat of Napoleon. What better instrument for the promotion of the idea of nationalism and a new morality. But the power struggle between the ruling élite and the new urban bourgeoisie remained unresolved. Instead the web of relations between the City and the West End, the enfranchised and the disenfranchised, became ever more complex with the question of authority continually to the fore. And it was only after the 1832 Reform Act that these fissures in the make-up of the nation began to close.

Notes

1.   The concept of nationalism seems to have emerged at the end of the eighteenth century. The French writers G. de Bertier Sauvigny and Abbé Barnel used the term in the late 1790s. But it did not come into common parlance in Europe until the end of the nineteenth century.

2.   Karl Deutsch, *Nation and Society*, Cambridge, Mass., MIT, 1966, 96–8, 101, 104–5 esp.

3.   Richard Crutwell, *Remarks on the Buildings and Improvements in London and Elsewhere*, London, 1816, 35.

4.   E. Hobsbawn (ed.) 'Inventing Tradition' in *The Invention of Tradition*, Cambridge, Cambridge University Press, 1983, 13–14.

5.   William Hazlitt, 'On Londoners and Country People', *The Plain Speaker*, 1836.

6.   See 'Report of the Select Committee on the British Museum', Parliamentary Papers, 1836, 444ff.

7.   Richard Crutwell *op. cit.*, 39.

8.   Royal Academy Council Minute Book, 1813–18, 5, 240.

9.   Linda Colley, *Britons: the forging of a nation*, New Haven and London, Yale University Press, 1992.

10. The 1774 Building Acts are fully discussed in J. Summerson, *Georgian London*, Harmondsworth, Penguin, 1978.

11. On this point see D. Olsen, *Town Planning in London*, New Haven and London, Yale University Press, 1982.

12. *The Picture of London*, 3rd edn, London, 1815, 159–60.

13. Ibid., 158–9.

14. S. and R. Percy, *The Percy History and Interesting memorial on the rise, progress and present state of all the capitals of Europe*, 3 vols, London, 1823, II, 343.

15. For a full discussion of class in relation to the city see Chapter 5.

16. This phenomenon is discussed in L. Colley *op. cit.*

17. For a fuller discussion of the ways in which the middle and upper classes were taught to view the landscape see M. Andrews, 'A Picturesque Template: the Tourists and their guidebooks' in D. Arnold (ed.) *The Picturesque in late Georgian England*, London, The Georgian Group, 1995.

18. Price published follow-on volumes to his *Essay on the Picturesque*, 1792 as *Essays on the Picturesque*, London, 1794. This quotation appears in volume I, p. 39.

19. From a letter from Repton to Uvedale Price Esq. London 1794 in J. C. Loudon, *The Landscape Gardening and Landscape Architecture of the late Humphry Repton Esq. being his entire works on these subjects*, London, 1840, 106.

20. *London Lions for Country Cousins and Friends about Town, New Buildings, improvements and amusements in the British Metropolis Illustrated with wood engravings by Horace Wellbeloved*, London, 1826, 20 and 22.

21. S. and R. Percy *op. cit.*, III, 355.

22. John Williams, *An Historical Account of Subways*, London, 1828, v–vi.

23. See HKW, 647.

24. S. and R. Percy *op. cit.*, III, 211.

25. 1833 Committee on Public Walks, 5.

26. Richard Crutwell *op. cit.*, iii.

27. Many of these plans – some of them quite improbable – are outlined in F. Barker and R. Hyde, *London as it Might Have Been*, London, John Murray, 1982.

28. This was exhibited at the Royal Academy in 1816 (no. 827).

29. For a full discussion of the sculptural monuments to the Napoleonic Wars see A. Yarrington, *The Commemoration of the Hero 1800–1864: monuments to the British victors of the Napoleonic Wars*, New York and London, Garland Press, 1988.

30. On this point see H. Colvin (ed.) *The History of the King's Works*, VI, London, HMSO, 1972, 293–297.

31. A full discussion of the sculptural decoration of Marble Arch appears in HKW *op. cit.*, 293–7.

32. See appendix HKW *op. cit.*, 300–301.

33. Flaxman died before work began but the question of suitable drapery is discussed in his letter BM Add MS 39781, f.254–5.

34. These are fully discussed in A. Yarrington *op. cit.*

35. G. Bataille, *The Accursed Share, an essay on general economy*, trans. R. Hurley, New York, Zone, 1991.

36. The attempts to commemorate the military achievements of the Duke of Wellington discussed within the paradigm of Bataille's notion of sacrifice form the basis of my forthcoming essay 'If only the Duke of Wellington had died at Waterloo! The problems of commemorating a hero in the absence of sacrifice' in A. Ballantyne (ed.) *Architecture and Sacrifice*.

37. S. and R. Percy *op. cit.*, II, 130.

4

The Theory of Police

The formation of the modern state had power or authority as its core and the early nineteenth-century metropolis was an ideal location for the development and exercise of these systems of control. The rise of a substantial urban middle class enabled the increasing bureaucratic structures by supplying both the workforce necessary for their implementation and the common will for such systems of control. This authority was expressed through London's architecture and urban planning as well as through the social rituals and cultural practices of its populace. This kind of rationality, implemented in the exercise of power, is explained by Foucault who identified two sets of precepts which dated from the sixteenth century: the *reason of state* and the *theory of police*.[1] These doctrines referred to two separate articulations of power: political power over legal subjects and pastoral power wielded over individuals. *Reason of state* concerns those acts of governing which reinforce the state and its institutions as such and to enable this precise quantifiable information about the strength of the state is required. Foucault referred to this kind of knowledge as *political statistics* or *arithmetic*. In this way the notion of the theory of police is much broader than the present day understanding of the police force, it refers instead to the technology of government which located the techniques and targets of state intervention. This required minutely detailed knowledge of the state's resources and identified for the first time the populace as a discrete entity which could be quantified in terms of fertility and mortality rates. These attitudes shaped the urban experience of Londoners through the complex sets of social relationships between classes and the assertion of authority by national and civic bodies through the performance of ritual and innovations in urban planning. These elements cohered in a notion of the state which was closely related to the idea of the nation of London. But nationhood was part of the more abstract image of the metropolis whereas the state comprised recognisable procedural apparatus.

In the realms of the census

The introduction of the census in 1801 is a prime example of this concern for *arithmetic*. For the first time attention was paid to the lives and conduct of individuals in terms of their abilities, morality and well-being. The population was securely mapped according to place of residence, volume of occupants per dwelling and their gender and occupation. The statistical analysis of the metropolis, and indeed the country as a whole, went beyond the collation of information for governmental institutions as it informed the texts of the many guidebooks and histories of London which appeared in the opening decades of the nineteenth century. The presentation of the 'rational' city in this popular format reinforced these kinds of power system as it presented London's unknowable entirety in terms of comprehensible, compartmentalised statistics. The three volume *Percy History*, published in 1823 and dedicated to George IV, wished to

present in methodical form those memorials which illustrate the rise, progress and present state of London and point out how an industrious people has preserved their liberties against foreign and domestic invasion and raised the city to a rank which is unparalleled amongst other nations.[2]

The text offered a detailed population analysis, based on the first three censuses, of the cities of London and Westminster and the Borough of Southwark. Specific attention was paid to the class of citizen, indicated by the nature of their employment (see Table 4.1). Percy's analysis demonstrated how the census offered an insight and understanding of the metropolis that had not previously been possible and this *arithmetic* was the basis of both national and civic power structures.

The data on the metropolis was not always based on the information gathered from the census, empirical observation also played its part. William Darton's *A Description of London* (1824), subtitled 'a sketch of the history and present state [of London] and almost all the celebrated public buildings', gives a comprehensive account of the metropolis including its shape and infrastructure and a range of detailed statistics. The information about the size, internal divisions and streets of London emphasises the city's vastness – Darton counts no less than 8000 streets, lanes, alleys and courts and 70 squares. This expanse was made knowable through Darton's comprehensive statistical analysis of urban experience and the possibilities for social life which included information on the provision of foodstuff, places of public

Table 4.1   Population of London based on the 1801, 1811 and 1821 censuses

London	City within the walls	City without the walls including the Inns of Court and Chancery	City and Liberties of Westminster	The Borough of Southwark
Houses	11,571	9,232	18,502	12,477
Houses building	32	73	391	208
Houses uninhabited	560	455	382	502
Families	56,174	16,497	41,558	21,207
Men	27,506	34,441	85,082	41,690
Women	28,668	34,819	97,003	44,215
Employed in agriculture	2	55	308	272
Employed in trade or manufacture	9,609	11,592	25,126	15,075
Employed in neither trade nor agriculture (i.e. not in either class)	1,960	4,850	16,120	5,860

Source: S. and R. Percy, *The Percy History and Interesting memorial on the rise, progress and present state of all the capitals of Europe*, London, 1823

Table 4.2   Darton's statistics on London

Provisions eaten annually

Acres of ground for vegetable growing near the metropolis	10,000
Acres of ground for fruit growing near the metropolis	3,000
Flesh markets	25
Corn and hay markets	25

Places of public worship

Churches of established religions	122
Chapels of each established religion	67
Foreign Protestant churches and chapels	19
Roman Catholic chapels	15
Synagogues for the Jews	6
Dissenters Chapels	190
Total	419

Table 4.2   *concluded*

Public literary and charitable institutions

Free schools	45
Public companies	94
Seminaries for education including 237 charitable schools	4,254
Societies for promoting good morals	8
Societies for promoting the learned useful and polite arts	12
Royal and national institutions for the advancement of polite arts and letters	5
Colleges for various uses	3
Public Libraries	18
Literary Institutions	6
National museum	1
Hospitals and dispensaries	52
Alms houses and asylums	122
Benefit and friendly societies	784
Institutions for educating the poor on the plan of Mr Lancaster and Dr Bull	30

Places of public amusement

Royal theatres: Drury Lane and Covent Garden open 1 October – end of June

Opera House for Italian Opera and French Ballet open winter to mid-summer

Several subscription concerts

Vauxhall Gardens open mid-May until the end of August

Haymarket theatre open end of June to the beginning of October

Lyceum theatre open end of June to the beginning of October

Sadlers Wells especially for aquatic exhibitions open Easter Monday to October

Davis's Amphitheatre for equestrian performances and pantomimes open as above

Amphitheatre of the Arts

Royal Circus or Surrey theatre (same openings as Sadlers Wells)

Coburg Theatre as above

Sans Pareil or Adelphi and some private theatres

Bartholomew Fair annually

Source: William Darton, *A Description of London: a sketch of the history and present state [of London] and almost all the celebrated public buildings,* 1824

worship, public literary and charitable institutions and places of amusement, all of which combine to present a rationalised, intelligible whole (see
Tables 4.1 and 4.2). The inclusion of the different theatre seasons also gave a
sense of time to the representation of the metropolis. Specific areas of London
were also subject to similar scrutiny as seen in R. Dobie's detailed analysis of
Bloomsbury (see Table 3.1, p. 50).[3]

National versus civic authority

The nineteenth-century metropolis provided an appropriate arena for the
display of different kinds of power system. But whose authority was this?
The fractured nature of London represented the complexity of the interrela-
tionship between the constituents parts: the cities of London and Westminster
and the Borough of Southwark. This reveals tensions within the power
structures and the kinds of mechanism used to implement these. Moreover,
the increasing use of rationality, as seen in the re-shaping of the built environment or the development of bureaucratic systems, brought with it an
important role for the bourgeoisie. In this way systems to represent the
power of the state facilitated an important shift in the governmental systems
of social control, not least the rise and proliferation of the civil service,
staffed largely by the new middle classes. London provides a particularly
important example of the role of the bourgeoisie in the social and political
equation as the internal dynamic between the City, which represented the
disenfranchised yet financially and commercially vital middle class, and the
state, which represented the ruling elite including the government and
the monarch, presented a fractured power system. The 1832 Reform Act
widened the franchise and went some way towards bridging this divide but
for many it was seen as not far reaching enough.

The City of London was a discrete entity within the metropolis. It represented the financial and commercial interests of London and the country
and had originally formed most of the capital city. The Corporation of London administered the business activities and acted as a kind of local
government with the Lord Mayor, elected annually, as its principal official.
The Lord Mayor was head of the oldest municipal corporation in the world.
Within the City of London he ranked before everyone except the sovereign.
This status underlined the autonomy of the City and the status of its elected
leader within its own jurisdiction. Outside the City the Lord Mayor still
enjoyed considerable status, ranking immediately after the Privy Council-
lors. The City of Westminster had a more complex structure. It was at once
the site of national government and the London residence of the monarch –
the head of state. Across the river in the Borough of Southwark the popula-

tion was mostly artisanal and was therefore disengaged from the ongoing dialectic of the civic and national authorities. The differing natures of these two areas and their perceived significance is expressed by William Darton: 'The west end of town from Charing cross is the most modern and elegant part of London inhabited by the court, nobility and gentry and is the seat of government.' Whereas, he continues, 'Southwark is chiefly inhabited by merchants and traders'.[4]

There was social and political friction between the cities of London and Westminster in the years directly preceding the 1832 Reform Act. Parliament was made up of only the very upper end of society – the ruling élite. The City, although represented in this body, comprised mainly middle and merchant classes who stood outside of the area of national government because of their social caste. During the opening decades of the nineteenth century the metropolis became an instrument of the governmental system. The rationalisation of street plans and the concerns for the well-being of trade and the populace were hallmarks of this.[5] The Metropolitan Improvements which were such a vital part of the creation of a modern metropolis were implemented with all the clout of a government project with state funding. The creation of a rationalised urban environment and not least the construction of an effective road and sewer system were underpinned by the government's ability to raise revenue by taxation and to use this to stamp its authority on the cityscape.

The City of London and its civic system had long been seen as representative of a kind of republicanism.[6] Expressions of anti-establishment feeling and the wish for egalitarianism became increasingly frequent in the period 1760–1830 and the City was a regular location for such demonstrations. The City authorities were not always in sympathy with the specific activities of those who demonstrated on their doorstep even if both parties shared a common concern for the right to vote. But the independent nature of the City and its symbolic identity as a body able to make a stand against national government made it an attractive location for expressions of dissent. John Wilkes is an early case in point. Wilkes campaigned to be MP for the City in order to further the case for universal male suffrage. His eventual election as MP for Middlesex in 1768 was a victory for the cause. Celebrations by Wilkes' mainly working-class supporters took place in the City. The Corporation did not share the mob's enthusiasm which resulted in the windows of the Mansion House being smashed.[7]

The French Revolution both heightened and relieved tensions between the City and the West End. The struggle for equality and the vote remained hard fought and the demonstrated power of the London mob, based principally in the older parts of the city, remained a continual reminder to government of the powerful potential of the populace. The assassination of the Prime

4.1   George Cruikshank, Poor John Bull – The Free Born Englishman – Deprived of his Seven Senses by the Six New Acts?, 1819. Engraving

Minister, Mr Spencer Perceval, in the House of Commons on 11 May 1812 by John Bellingham was a shocking act. But the unrest continued, resulting in the suspension of the Act of Habeas Corpus followed by the Six Acts which gave the state tighter control (Figure 4.1). The disenfranchised middle classes were undeterred and in 1820 a plot to murder several members of the cabinet, including the Duke of Wellington, was foiled and resulted in five executions. The estranged spouse of George IV, Queen Caroline, became a figurehead for those who were dissatisfied with the status quo. Riots and demonstrations – even by members of the army – during the hapless queen's abortive trial for adultery in 1820 raised the political temperature further still.[8]

The City authorities did not wholeheartedly take up the cause of enfranchisement. But the wealthy merchants and businessmen became increasingly agitated at their lack of political power. The dynamic between the central, national government and the City was a complex set of relationships centring on civic pride and the financial autonomy of the City's institutions, which covered all manner of trades as well as banking. The financial and commercial institutions were nationally important and enabled government policy through taxation and loans. They were part of the identity of London and the nation as a whole. By 1830 the resentment at the government's failure to widen the franchise had reached a volatile level. As a result, in November of that year William IV declined his traditional invitation to attend the annual Lord Mayor's Banquet. The Prime Minister, Sir Robert Peel, had advised against it as the frequent anti-government riots and demonstrations which were taking place in the City compromised the king's safety.[9] And the Duke of Wellington was told that his presence at the banquet would have been 'likely to create a disturbance, for the consequences of which the authorities of the City would not answer'.[10] The cities of Westminster and London were indeed in opposition.

Ritual authority: reinventing traditions

The City was then a site for the expression of social and political ideals which challenged national systems. But how did it maintain its image of authority and independence as the neighbouring City of Westminster, the home of national government, became increasingly dominant? The isolated grandeur of its key buildings no doubt helped embellish the authority of the City. But it was the public performance of institutional rituals which underpinned the Corporation of London's local hegemony and the national significance of the City. Most notable amongst these was the Lord Mayor's Show. This remains a piece of street theatre which presents a sort of tradition borne out of ritual which fed off the 'absent' presence of the monarchy in eighteenth-century London as court life, such as it was, had been focused on the royal residences on the western periphery of the capital.[11] The incoming Lord Mayor took his oath of office before the Judges of the King's or Queen's bench.[12] The show was his procession to this event and was bound up in the display of ritual and tradition that helped create the aura of authority. The purpose of this symbolic act was for the Lord Mayor to swear 'fealty' to the Crown. The show comprised a great parade which represented the mercantile and cultural prowess of the City. This had risen to such an extent that in 1841 an East India Company ship drawn by six horses formed part of the procession. By the mid-eighteenth century the Lord Mayor no longer processed on horseback but was conveyed in a grand coach designed by the architect Robert Taylor. The painted decorations depicted the City's achievements and standing as a centre of trade and commerce, and its wealth. St Paul's Cathedral features prominently as an image not only of the City's piety but also of the City itself. And it is not without irony that this spectacle of civic independence and egalitarianism was itself a means of social and

4.2   The Mansion House, from the Bank, 1829. Engraving

political control. Hazlitt observed that the sense of contrived community gave a feeling of common ownership:

[the true cockney, i.e. typical Londoner] meets the Lord Mayor's coach, and without ceremony treats himself to an imaginary ride in it. He notices the people going to court or to a city-feast, and is quite satisfied with the show.[13]

By the early 1830s the nature of the parade had taken on a deeper significance. The men in mock armour who accompanied the Lord Mayor were perhaps too suggestive of a potentially liberating force. This together with the fact that the City was seen as a focus for opposition to the Crown led to the cancellation of the show until after the 1832 Reform Act.

The Lord Mayor's official residence, the Mansion House (Figure 4.2), acted as a kind of court providing opulent receptions for visiting dignitaries paid for by the Corporation of London, as one guest noted:

This [the Lord Mayor's dinner] took place today in the Guildhall. ... It lasted full six hours, and six hundred people were present. The tables were set parallel from top to bottom of the hall, with the exception of one which was placed across it, at the top. At this the Lord Mayor and his most distinguished guests were seated ... the vast hall and its lofty columns ... the huge mirrors ... the brilliant illumination turned night into day ... . The toasts ... were all of a national character. ... The Lord Mayor made twenty-six speeches [and] a foreign diplomate also ventured upon one.[14]

The Mansion House and the civic rituals performed there presented an image of an alternative, more democratic governmental structure. Here the annual Lord Mayor's Banquet was a key political event both for the City and the government where key ministers were invited to speak on government policy.[15]

The connection between the two Cities is expressed in ritualistic terms by Temple Bar – the formal gateway into the City from the west. Robert Southey describes the kind of political ritual practised at this highly significant geographical location on the signing of the Treaty of Amiens which was supposed to bring peace between Britain and France:

> The theory of the ceremony ... founded upon a fiction, is, that the Lord Mayor of London, and the people of London ... being wholly ignorant of what has been going on, the king sends officially to acquaint them that he has made peace: accordingly that gates at Temple Bar, which divided London and Westminster, and which stand open day and night, are on this occasion closed; and garter, king-at-arms, with all his heraldic peers, rides up to them and knocks loudly for admittance. The Lord Mayor, mounted on a charger, is ready on the other side to demand who is there. King Garter then announces himself and his errand and requires permission to pass and proclaim the good news; upon which the gates are thrown open.[16]

The rituals surrounding the authority of the City of Westminster were far more diverse and less symbolic of the kind of power and authority enjoyed by the Lord Mayor. The Coronation of the Monarch was perhaps the apogee of spectacle and display of the aura of authority. George IV's coronation was perhaps the most opulent and lavish ever seen in Britain. Not only was there a grand procession but the pageantry of the ritual banquet in Westminster Hall was revived and performed for the benefit of the court, the government and attending dignitaries. Royal weddings and funerals were less opulent and, for certain members of the royal family, were not necessarily state occasions.[17] After this court life had its well-established protocols and traditions but these remained mostly invisible to the populace at large. But the powerful combination of state and monarch in the State opening of Parliament was the surest signifier of national power structures. The monarch processes from the royal residence (from the mid-1820s this was Buckingham Palace) through the Mall and Whitehall. But the constitutional nature of the monarchy is clearly evident in the speech given to open Parliament which set out the *government's* agenda. Tradition had to be invented here as the absence of presence of the monarchy in eighteenth-century London meant the urban landscape had remained essentially domestic with few public buildings and no grand royal palace. Moreover, as George III had been an unostentatious monarch there was little in terms of public pomp or ceremony during his reign. Visibility and conspicuous display of authority was now crucial. The newly laid out and revamped Royal Parks afforded processional routes for the performance of recently invented or revived institutional rituals or to facilitate royal attendance at the mock battles and military parades held in Hyde Park. The pageantry of monarchical authority extended to the metropolitan road system. Up until the last quarter of the eighteenth century the network of private royal roads through and out of London had survived. These roads ran mainly to the south-west of the city providing access to the royal palaces of Hampton Court and Kew, and Richmond Park with its hunting lodge.[18] But this private infrastructure was gradually eroded not least due to the cost of maintaining these thoroughfares. The Hampton Court Road and the Richmond Road were gradually opened to the public and their costs defrayed by local ratepayers. The Fulham Road remained nominally private and served as a processional route from Buckingham House via Pimlico, Chelsea and Fulham to Kew. But as London spread west the pressure to open up this road, not least to allow the development of Belgravia to accommodate the court, now established around Buckingham House, became too much.[19] And, certainly, the role of the Metropolitan Improvements in the production of roads, infrastructures and public open spaces was essential in enabling the performance of the rituals of authority.

Aggressive authority

The ritual of authority was complemented by a tightening of social control in the metropolis, a kind of internal aggression. One of the principal prompts for the tightening of structures of control were the Gordon Riots of 1780, a 50,000 strong protest aginst the repeal of the anti-Roman Catholic legislation led by Lord George Gordon, when over 850 lost their lives and many of London's key buildings – including Downing Street and the Bank of England – were besieged. Up until this time there had been no coherent police force, in the modern sense of the word, in London. There had been various systems implemented which were specific to either the City or Westminster. But these relied on the middle classes to act as officers and support the role of the aggressive authorities. Many constables, as they were known, in both the City and Westminster were in sympathy with the demands of the Gordon Rioters and did nothing to stop their destructive path. Despite this disarray the Police Bill of 1785 did little to improve the situation. It attempted to unify the policing of the cities of London and Westminster and the Borough of Southwark and was seen as such a bad idea that it was never implemented. The most locally coherent and effective methods of policing came from the City merchants and were designed to protect their property. In 1798 a river police force was formed to stop piracy and theft from traders with the

West Indies who were based in the new docks. This proved so successful that the scheme was taken over by the state and the Thames Police was founded to protect all the traders who relied on the Thames. The roads, another vital artery in the distribution of goods, were also protected by a City organization – the Bow Street horse patrol – established in 1805. This resulted in the paradoxical situation in the early nineteenth century of the City of London, with little more than 10 per cent of the population of London, having nearly half of the total police force of the capital. In real terms this meant that by 1822 the Home Secretary had around 400 officers or constables on whom he could call to control a population of around one million. But there was strong public and parliamentary opposition to the increase in the police proposed by the Home Secretary Robert Peel as it would lead to greater loss of freedom, and the loudest objections came from the City. Not only were they well protected by their own organisations but they were opposed to placing police powers in the hands of a government which remained unreformed and in which they had no role. Peel's Metropolitan Police Bill of 1829 had been a tactical success as it excluded the City and the Bow Street and Thames Police, who retained their separate identity and authority. This continued for a further decade although the Bill did nothing to quell the vigorous and growing opposition to both Peel and Wellington. The political prize of the vote and the power this would give to the bourgeoisie, including many City merchants and traders, became an increasingly important issue prompting much civil unrest. And the Reform Riots of 1831 were a vigorous manifestation of social and political discontent. Even with their new political power after the 1832 Reform Act the City merchants retained some autonomy as the City of London Police was formed in 1839, its jurisdiction confined to the square mile.

Although a coherent and effective police force evaded the state for much of the early nineteenth century the army was also at its disposal as a signifier of its power. The building of new and the repositioning of old barracks was an essential part of the Metropolitan Improvements. But the importance of a strong military presence had been appreciated before this time. The Gordon Riots were suppressed by the army even though this was disapproved of by C. J. Fox, Edmund Burke and even the Whig government. And, subsequently, barracks were built to prevent a reoccurrence of civil disorder.[20] This trend continued with the inclusion of new barracks in the plan for the Regent's Park. Charing Cross had also been the site of a temporary barracks. These were adjacent to William Kent's Royal Stables (1732). As part of the general improvements of the area many of the near derelict buildings which made up the area known as 'The Royal Mews' were demolished to leave the Royal Stables standing as a suitable terminus at the top of Whitehall (Figure 4.3).[21] The barracks were rebuilt in 1825 providing new accommodation for 800

THE KING'S MEWS, CHARING CROSS.

4.3   The Royal Stables, Charing Cross, 1829. Engraving

troops further to the north behind the Royal Stables which were demolished a few years later to make way for the National Gallery. As the Master of Fortification stated 'it gave free access from the back of the barracks to all the North Parts of the town'[22] and facilitated the movement of troops across the city (Figure 4.4). The social and aesthetic changes to Charing Cross in the opening decades of the nineteenth century are minutely described by one observer in the mid-1830s:

The state of London may be somewhat guessed at by a short description of the fine open street from the statue at Charing Cross to the commencement of Parliament Street. [In previous times] … The place could not be outdone in infamy and indecency by any place in London. The manner in which many of the drunken, filthy young prostitutes behaved is not describable nor would it be believed were it described. … It seems almost incredible that such a street could be in the condition described, but so it was: people were not then offended with the grossness, dirtiness, vulgarity, obscenity and atrocious language. … I need hardly notice how highly respectable the street is now.[23]

The area around Charing Cross which was full of densely packed rookeries had seemed ungovernable and impossible to police but the aggressive assertion of authority achieved the desired transformation. After the brutality of the French Revolution, where the power of the mob was all too evident, the primary concern in the opening years of the nineteenth century was the protection of the hegemony of the ruling élite who dominated both the metropolis and the country as a whole. Opposition to this system gathered

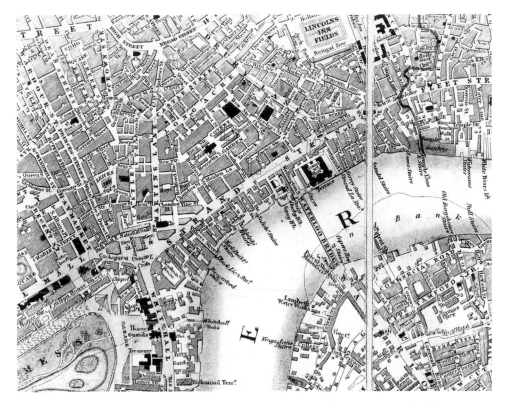

4.4   Cruchley's Map showing Charing Cross (the Royal Academy was never built), *c.* 1830

pace in the years 1800–1840 as the middle classes became increasingly active in their pursuit of the right to vote.[24] One of the principal executants of the resistance to the demand for enfranchisement was the Duke of Wellington. He joined the government after his victory at Waterloo and his first years in politics coincided with civil unrest and a struggle for democratic rights for which he had no sympathy.[25] The tactics he used to suppress these were harshly repressive. Wellington's actions were reminiscent of his military campaigns against the French, here turned on the British in his new role as prime minister. This resulted in an unacceptable use of militaristic and imperialistic methods against the populace. The suspension of the Act of Habeas Corpus in 1818 facilitated the detention of dissenters and the Six Acts, a series of laws in 1819 which restricted freedom of speech and other civil liberties, tightened further state authority and control. Moreover, the Peterloo Massacre, when troops turned on and killed demonstrators for democracy in Manchester, was not named by chance – as an act of repression committed internally rather than externally it was seen as a massacre rather than a victory.[26]

Building authority

The Metropolitan Improvements and associated developments in London sought to assert the authority of the state in two main ways. First, in the building of new barracks and the crucial placing of troops in the capital to allow more aggressive forms of social control. And more importantly, the assertion of the authority of the state and through it the nation's safety which redefined the relationship of the individual to the state. This was achieved through the new street planning; the strategic placing of monuments; new public buildings and the opening up of the Royal Parks to create public open spaces in the capital. These elements redefined the nature of urban experience in an attempt to create a unified national identity which represented these systems of authority.

The re-imaging of London began with John Nash's plan for the development of London, which was presented under three main headings: *Utility to the Public, Beauty of the Metropolis* and *Practicability*. It is not without irony that French architecture influenced his ideas about planning and architectural design. This can be seen, for instance, in the relationship between Mansart's long façades at Versailles and the terraces at La Place de la Concorde in Paris and Nash's scheme for long terraces in the Regent's Park (Figure 4.5). French rationalist theory as seen in the work of architects like Charles Nicolas Ledoux, whose imaginary *Ville Ideale de Chaux* (1804) contained public

4.5   John Nash, Cumberland Terrace, Regent's Park, 1827. Engraving

parks in which were situated monuments to amongst other things the Cult of Moral Values and the New Ethics, was also very influential for town planning. The development of the public urban space which could be park-land or part of the urban streetscape was an essential ingredient in the self-conscious construction of authority. The importance of place in this new urban environment is revealed in the development of the area now called Trafalgar Square. Until about 1820 Charing Cross (as it was previously called) was the gate to Whitehall and the Royal Park of St James. In many ways the creation of Trafalgar Square can be seen as an enlargement of the forecourt in front of these gates – before it was named Trafalgar Square there was a proposal to call it King's Square.

This entrance way had been the most important land entrance to Whitehall, the river approach to it being the most significant. It had been used as an approach to the seat of government by returning armies or packs of dissidents. During the civil war hangings, beheadings, and drawings and quarterings regularly took place and the majority of the regicides were ex-ecuted here. Charles I was executed within the perceived royal precinct a few hundred yards down the road at the Banqueting House. Displays of brutality continued at this spot. In the first half of the eighteenth century branding, nose splitting and ear lopping were regular occurrences. In 1703 Daniel Defoe had stood in the public pillory for three days. He, however, was not stoned to death but bedecked with flowers whilst his 'Hymn to the Pillory' was eagerly purchased by the crowd.

By the Regency period these practices had been replaced by more subtle expressions of authority and power. The displacement of the poorer ele-ments of the population to enable the building of the new street is an obvious manifestation and the subsequent zoning of classes confirmed the state's authority. But the new symbols of the state dotted across the metropolis were the main method of reinforcing the state's power. This was certainly more subtle than public execution or mutilation on the king's doorstep.

In 1826 Nash published a plan to build a Royal Academy based on a Greek temple in the centre of the space and proposed that a National Gallery of Art should be situated at Charing Cross (Figure 4.4).[27] This was intended to accompany the proposed circular doric temple to be placed in Piccadilly Circus as a monument to Shakespeare. William Wilkins' National Gallery (1834–8) replaced Kent's Royal Mews – a fitting symbol of different manifes-tations of authority. These schemes for Charing Cross were intended to link with Robert Smirke's British Museum, another symbol of the nation's prow-ess through its collection of antiquities, begun in 1823. They were to be connected to Charing Cross via an axial road leading directly from the museum's main entrance.[28] In this way authority became more symbolic and the sense of shared community and belonging engendered by the City

4.6   William Railton, Design for the Nelson Monument in front of the National Gallery, Trafalgar Square, *c.* 1838

rituals was transposed into the built environment of the West End. The final politicisation of this space came a decade later when Railton's great column was erected in honour of Lord Admiral Nelson (Figure 4.6).

The absent presence of the monarchy in the preceding century was particularly felt in the architecture of the metropolis. Attempts to right this and to reaffirm the significance of the capital as the seat of both royal and state authority were manifest in the continuous remodelling of Carlton House and extravagant plans for Buckingham Palace.[29] And these two worlds collided with Sir John Soane's Royal Entrance to the House of Lords (1822–7) which was the end point of the king's processional route to parliament.[30] The prodigious growth in the number of public buildings whether they be governmental offices like Soane's New State Paper Office (1830–4) or Sir Robert Smirke's General Post Office (1824–9), reinforced the modern image of the metropolis and signified the ever-encroaching administrative systems which underpinned its authority and power. Even Decimus Burton's Parliamentary Mews (1825–6) had an authoritarian air about it. But it was generally agreed by writers and guidebooks on London that the metropolis lacked the kind of architectural grandeur found in other European capitals. *The Ambulator* remarked that 'The magnificence of royalty is not to be found in the palaces of the metropolis' and goes on to list the principal buildings in St James's as having 'no architectural distinction'.[31]

The authority and prestige of the Corporation of London found physical expression in the grand architecture of the Mansion House (*c*. 1740–50) by George Dance the elder.[32] Similarly the importance of trade and commerce were represented in the rebuilding of the Bank of England by Sir John Soane in the 1790s and the Royal Exchange by Sir William Tite in the 1840s.[33] And, not least, St Paul's Cathedral, perhaps London's most enduring symbol, stands in the City. The size, scale and splendour of these edifices equalled the grand public building projects of the West End. There is also no doubt that the rebuilding of London Bridge was seen to be as symbolic of the City's status as any of the other large building projects. But here, the part funding of the work by the state threatened the hegemony of the Corporation of London. Yet this predominantly classically styled, Augustan built environment is only one signifier of social and political pre-eminence; it sits between the equally important factors of ritual and experience.

Experiential authority

The power of the British Empire and the emerging status of London as a world city were symbolised in the landscaping of the Royal Parks. The redefined relationship between the residents of London – the flâneur/euse who walked and experienced the streets and parks – and the re-shaped urban landscape is important here. The metropolis was viewed by its publics through a range of scopic regimes some of which related to the templates for viewing formulated by the writers of the picturesque movement. The picturesque theorists had established the symbolic and narrative functions of landscape and architecture and the public was used to reading them in this way. Here, this language was being used in the service of the state as opposed to an individual landowner and its metropolitan context made it all the more potent. The monuments that engendered feelings of nationalism also played an important part in the assertion of the power of the state.[34] The new system of roads, punctuated with monuments, impressive public buildings and culminating in a new royal residence offered the well-to-do residents of London a feeling of safety. And every Londoner was invited to celebrate the nation's security, thanks to the king, through the memorials and triumphal archways strategically placed in the Royal Parks to which there was now public access.

The design and layout of the parks were seen as a two-way contract – creating a sense of public well-being, edification and peace in these public open spaces. The sense of common ownership and careful presentation of symbols of monarchy and state were an important part of the planning behind the Metropolitan Improvements in London. Here polite society could be seen and see each other thanks to the munificence of the state. By contrast the garden square and privately owned gardens were jealously guarded by residents and were not open to any visitors regardless of social class. This was remarked upon by visitors to the capital including Prince Pückler-Muskau – 'the grudging inhumanity with which the opulent classes shut up their charming pleasure-grounds' he attributed to 'the moroseness of the rich [which] it is difficult for people on the Continent to imagine'.[35]

The Regent's Park project and the Royal Parks stand distinct from these well-established signifiers of social exclusion of the urban landscape. Here the villa garden was an essential part of the development of the cityscape into a more generally available consumable space. It provided both a physical and visual link between private and public parkland and was a conduit through which the ideologies of the picturesque movement could be distilled into a metropolitan context. The landscaping of the villas' grounds and approaches had an important effect on the overall appearance of the park as the villas and their gardens were integrated into the whole rather than being defined as separate precincts through the use of walls or tall hedges and fences. But the park was not without its critics. John Claudius Loudon, the influential landscape theorist, recognised the division between these different kinds of urban landscape when he commented on the design of the Regent's Park:

But in 1810 Regent's park commenced from a suggestion by William Fordyce Esq late Surveyor of Woods and Forests and it promises to be a scene worthy of a metropolis. It is only regretted that the space available to the public is so much curtailed by interspersed villas, and surrounding houses and gardens – for though from the number of trees, the wealthy citizen who can view the scenery from his house or coach may recognize the park character, yet by rendering so great an extent of the surface private property, the wanderings of the pedestrian are limited and his view of the scenery confined.

Hyde, St James's and Green Park surrounded the new royal palace and formed part of its grounds. As such they collectively constituted a landscape similar to that which surrounded country houses. The landscape of country houses had already been identified as containing a variety of meanings. And although these parks were in an urban setting the landscaping issues surrounding their improvement had resonance with the wider debates about landscape in the early nineteenth century. The use of landscape design principles to shape urban space offered a subtler reading of the cityscape than that presented by the abrupt class consciousness of developments like Regent Street.

Although the Royal Parks did little to enhance the image of George IV or his successor the advantages they gave to the general population was noted. The improved public open spaces of the Royal Parks had succeeded in providing enjoyment and pleasure to visitors of all classes. The importance of public open spaces was investigated by the select Committee on Public Walks of 1833. The report summarized many of the changes which had taken place in the London landscape in the previous 50 years. First, the population of the city had nearly tripled since 1750. Second, the report confirmed that over the preceding 50 years there had been a building boom and increase in property values that had led to many open spaces being enclosed. It also summarized the aims and achievements of the development of the Royal Parks and their status within the urban fabric.

St James's Park, Green Park and Hyde Park ... afford to the inhabitants of this Western portion of the Metropolis inestimable advantages as Public Walks. ... for this accommodation it is understood the Public are indebted to His present Majesty.[36]

But the emphasis on the significance of urban landscapes had subtly changed. Public access to these open spaces remained of paramount importance. The links between open land, fresh air and health came to the fore whilst the 'royal emphasis' diminished. Prince Pückler-Muskau made a telling observation in August 1827:

I daily inspect ... St James's Park. ... It is characteristic, that while the laws which protect private property are so strict that a man who climbs over a wall into a garden runs the risk of being hanged ... with the public, wherever they have a shadow of a claim, it is necessary to go to work as gingerly as you would with a raw egg. This park is the property of the Crown, but has been open to the public since remote ages; the Government does not dare to close it, even temporarily, notwithstanding the improvements that the King is now carrying on, (at the nation's cost, it is true).[37]

The beneficial effects and feeling of well-being experienced by the populace though the parks should, according to the Committee, be spread more evenly across London. Land owned either by the Crown or the Duchy of Cornwall was sought for public open spaces across London and other large cities. The benefits of these landscapes and the feeling of state generosity and national pride they engendered in the populace was considered a useful tool.[38] Alongside public walks the Committee recommended places for exercise and recreation for the humbler classes. Without this 'facility for regulated amusement … great mischief must arise'. Open places reserved for amusement would wean the humbler classes from drink, dog fights and boxing. Relaxation in rich and poor must be a spring to industry. A small admission charge to such areas was even suggested to defray costs in contrast to the huge amount of public funds used in the works in the Royal Parks.

The technology of government was ably developed and employed in London during the years 1800–1840. The tensions between the hegemony of the élitist old systems and the power structures which now required the bourgeoisie to ensure their efficacy created a different social and political landscape. The re-imaging of London is closely related to these fundamental changes and the *arithmetic* of the modern metropolis informed the revision and representing of social and political institutions and practices. The different expressions of power in London in the period 1800–1840 combined to confirm Foucault's analysis of *the reason of state* and *the theory of police*. The 1832 Reform Act may not have gone far enough for many but it did alter the kind of political power the state wielded over its legal subjects and its pastoral power over the individual. The changing set of social relationships in the metropolis is perhaps best typified by the 1834 Poor Law Reform Act. Here the responsibility for care for the disadvantaged was removed from the locality and replaced by an impersonal mechanical and arguably more 'efficient system' of the workhouse. Bentham's Panopticon with all its implications of surveillance was the favoured architectural model for this method of social control.

Notes

1. See M. Foucault, *Politics, Philosophy, Culture*, ed. L. D. Kritzman, New York, Routledge, 1988, 67 esp.

2. S. and R. Percy, *The Percy History and Interesting memorial on the rise, progress and present state of all the capitals of Europe*, 3 vols, London, 1823, I, i.

3. R. Dobie, *The History of the United Parishes of St Giles in the Field and St George Bloomsbury*, London, 1829.

4. William Darton, *A Description of London*, London, 1824, 8.

5. For a fuller discussion of the use of urban space as an instrument of governmental ideology see D. Arnold, 'Rationality, Safety and Power: the street planning of later Georgian London', *The Georgian Group Journal*, 1995.

6. This question is discussed in Iain McCalman, 'Ultra Radicalism and Convivial Debating Clubs in London, 1795–1838', *English Historical Review*, 1987. See also H. T. Dickinson, 'Radical Culture' in C. Fox (ed.) *London World City*, New Haven and London, Yale University Press, 1992, 209–25.

7. This incident and the career and significance of Wilkes to the process of parliamentary reform is discussed in P. Langford, *A Polite and Commercial People*, Oxford, Oxford University Press, 1989, 377 esp.

8. See J. Bryant, 'Caroline: ranger and royal wanderer' in D. Arnold (ed.) *Squanderous and Lavish Profusion: George IV his image and patronage of the arts*, London, The Georgian Group, 1995, 31–6.

9. R. L. Jones, *Reminiscences of the Public Life of Richard Lambert Jones Esq.*, London, 1863.

10. Ibid., 58.

11. For a discussion of the role of ritual and the invention of tradition see D. Cannadine, 'The Context, Performance and Meaning of Ritual: the British Monarchy and the "invention of tradition", c. 1820–1977' in E. Hobsbawm and P. Ranger (eds) *The Invention of Tradition*, Cambridge, Cambridge University Press, 1983.

12. This took place at Westminster Hall until 1881 when the ceremony moved to the Law Courts.

13. William Hazlitt, *The New Monthly Magazine*, August 1823.

14. E. M. Butler (ed.) *A Regency Visitor, The English Tour of Prince Puckler-Muskau Described in his letters 1826–1828*, Collins, London, 1957, letter dated 16 April 1827, 191.

15. This tradition continues today. The Mansion House speech delivered by the Chancellor of the Exchequer is used by the government to outline its financial policies.

16. Robert Southey, *Letters from England*, London, 1807.

17. These are discussed in HKW, 647–51.

18. For a fuller discussion of the King's private roads see HKW *op. cit.*, 653–5.

19. Ibid., 655.

20. 1796 witnessed great developments in the building of barracks in London. Prompted partly by the Gordon Riots a magazine was built in Hyde Park and a new barracks constructed on Knightsbridge.

21. New royal stables in Pimlico were planned as early as 1820. This prompted George IV to permit the demolition of the east and west parts of the old mews to allow the construction of a road to link Pall Mall to St Martin's, which effectively created the area later called Trafalgar Square.

22. PRO Cres 26/178.

23. Francis Place, 'The Street Charing Cross', *Autobiography*, 1835.

24. On this point see Iain McCalman *op. cit.*

25. For a discussion of the career of the Duke of Wellington see Norman Gash (ed.) *Wellington Studies in the Military and Political Career of the First Duke of Wellington*, Manchester University Press in association with the University of Southampton, 1990.

26. See R. J. White, *From Waterloo to Peterloo*, Harmondsworth, Penguin, 1968.

27. The history behind the building of the National Gallery at Trafalgar Square is discussed in R. Liscombe, *William Wilkins 1778–1839*, Cambridge, Cambridge University Press, 1980, ch. XII.

28. See note 18.

29. These projects are discussed in M. H. Port, 'The Homes of George IV' in D. Arnold (ed.) *Squanderous and Lavish Profusion: George IV, his image and patronage of the arts*, London, The Georgian Group, 1995, 23–30.

30. See HKW, 520–5.

31. *The Ambulator*, 1811, 7.

32. A thorough account of the building history of the Mansion House appears in S. Jeffery, *The Mansion House*, Chichester, The Corporation of London and Phillimore and Co., 1993.

33. There were similar tensions between national and local government in the rebuilding of the Royal Exchange. A detailed history of The Royal Exchange is given in A. Saunders (ed.), *The Royal Exchange*, London, London Topographical Society Publication No. 152, 1997.

34. For a fuller discussion of these see R. Barker and R. Hyde, *London as it Might Have Been*, London, John Murray, 1982.

35. E. M. Butler *op. cit.*, letter dated 8 April 1827, 244–5.

36. 1833 Committee on Public Walks, 5.

37. E. M. Butler *op. cit.*, letter dated 8 April 1827, 244.

38. 1833 Committee on Public Walks, 8.

5

Free-born Sons [and daughters] of Commerce

The bourgeoisie were an essential part of the modern metropolis and they played a vital role in the political power structures and the social rituals and cultural practices of urban life. This rise to prominence of such a social group might be seen as progress – part of the democratising process which included the long awaited 1832 Reform Act. But this teleological interpretation of the expansion of a specific social group within an established hierarchy of the nineteenth-century urban environment masks the static nature of that society. If progress is viewed rather as a process of adaptation to a complex range of circumstances where consumption and economic growth come to the fore in urban environments, the city becomes both an enabler of and a restrictive force on a specific social group. There is no doubt that the growth of the consumer society impacted on London as a site of both production and consumption and that the middle class was essential to this process of adaptation. This commodification of the city and its ultimate fetishisation as an object of desire deflects attention away from the ideals of the state and places emphasis instead on the leisured classes.[1] Urban culture in its broadest possible meaning then becomes the display of power and the early nineteenth-century metropolis becomes an assemblage of a deceptive array of symbols of authority and social rank. These symbols were part of the urban experience of London and were visible in architecture and urban planning seen from the dome of St Paul's or at street level. But the most important aspect of design in relation to class was the question of style. It is here that the petite bourgeoisie borrowed the attributes of the haute bourgeoisie and 'the pillars from Attic temples, Gothic cathedrals; and the arrogant palaces of the Italian City-States'[2] articulated the desires and aspirations of the metropolitan middle class. It is here that the parallel forces of national identity and systems of state converged around a new middle-class persona. But more than this, class, like the symbols of nationhood or state control, becomes a way of reading the urban topography – without which the city makes no sense. The self-conscious acknowledgement of class in the architectural systems of the city has already been seen in the rating of houses and the relationship of this to a coherent national identity. But beyond this the deliberate construction of a socially specific urban topography invades all aspects of town planning.

The most obvious example of this kind of self-conscious construction of an urban environment is the development of Regent Street, which remained a focal point of the metropolis. Here the flâneur/euse both paraded and was observed in an appropriate setting:

Regent Street which extends from Carlton House to Portland Place, though of varied architecture, some of which is not in good taste, is still a noble street, and leads to one of the greatest ornaments in the metropolis, the Regent's Park. ... This park is very beautiful with laid out grounds exhibiting a charming variety of lawns, lakes and shrubberies.[3]

Both the Regent's Park and Regent Street were financed and constructed according to the same capitalist methods used in the building of London since the beginning of the speculative development boom in the early eighteenth century. But this ad hoc system of urban planning and growth was used here for a more coherent restructuring of London and division of the social classes. Not least the scale of these two projects eclipsed any previous development. Regent Street was to be the longest in London and the Regent's Park as planned comprised the largest complete speculative development in terms of scope, acreage and volume of housing the city had yet seen.[4] The aspirations of the urban bourgeoisie in terms of their wish for impressive leasehold dwellings and willingness to speculate on property were essential instruments in the execution of these projects. And in return these new developments reinforced the bourgeoisification of the metropolis.

The new street created for the first time a strong north–south axis through the city and with it came a division of the classes. In cruder terms the upper echelons lived to the west of the new street in the smart new squares. Shopkeepers, craftsmen and the very poor lived to the east. John Nash who laid out the blueprint for the project made no secret of his objective to:

provide a boundary and complete separation between the Streets and Squares occupied by the nobility and gentry, and the narrow streets and meaner Houses occupied by the mechanics and the trading parts of the community.[5]

As Sir John Summerson has pointed out there were sound economic reasons for Nash's snobbery – better houses meant better occupants and better rents. Building through the poorer areas was cheaper and meant the existing good quality building in the West End could be retained. The new street achieved this kind of social division as on its completion Nash wrote:

my purpose was that the new street should cross the eastern entrance to all the streets occupied by the higher classes and to leave out to the east all the bad streets, and as a sailor would express himself to hug all the avenues that went to good streets.[6]

The new street certainly did create a physical barrier between the classes, displacing many tradespeople around Haymarket and completely ruining many businesses.[7] It also halted the spread of the rookeries which were impossible to police. In an attempt to ensure that the lower classes should not penetrate these new developments it was decreed that the new street and park

shall be open at all times to all his Majesties Subjects to pass and repass along the same (except ... Waggons, Carts, Drays or the vehicles for the carriage of goods, merchandise, manure soil or other articles, or Oxen Cows Horses or Sheep in any drove or droves.)[8]

This measure could be interpreted simply as a wish to improve the traffic flow through the West End of London and it certainly gives a flavour of the diversity of traffic in London. But the real motive is betrayed in the response to the traders in St James's market who petitioned for the right of access to the new street. In defence of his new social map Nash replied

No it would spoil the beauty of the plan entirely – for people riding up and down might see offal or something of that kind.[9]

In 1822 inhabitants of the parishes of St Martin's and St Anne's Soho also petitioned against the closure of 'the passage through the Royal Mews recently shut in the interests of public service'.[10] The closure is significant here as it had provided a convenient link for traders between Soho and Westminster – two areas of very different social make-up. But how did these areas of contrasting demography interface?

Life on the edge

Regent Street was the fundamental core or backbone of the middle-class presence in London and the zoning of classes was so abrupt that there was virtually no transition between areas. It served not only as a line of demarcation but also to protect the area to its west known as the West End. The spread of London westwards throughout the eighteenth century had left a trail of 'once grand' garden squares in its wake. By 1800 the area between Bloomsbury and the new street comprised a mixture of dwellings shops and small-scale manufacturing industries including coach makers, picture framers and print sellers. Although the Strand, which runs along the southern edge of this area, was improved in the 1810s (Figures 5.1 and 5.2) most of the

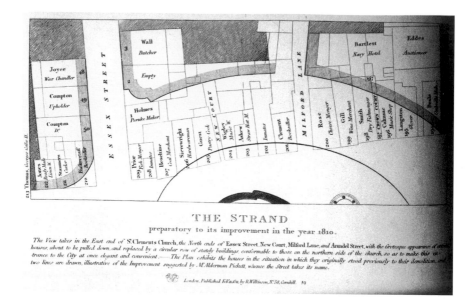

5.1   Ground plan of The Strand, preparatory to its improvement in the year 1810

5.2   Elevation of The Strand, preparatory to its improvement in the year 1810

HUNGERFORD MARKET, STRAND.

5.3   Hungerford Market, the Strand, 1829. Engraving

area remained a tangle of narrow streets like Hungerford Market which ran north–south intersecting the Strand at its southern end (Figure 5.3). Regent Street ring-fenced the squares to its west and offered some protection from the encroachment of the lower orders. This is not to say that the West End offered the kind of social homogeneity envisioned for the Regent's Park and Regent Street projects. There was a diversity of social class at the margins, not least the homes of the servants and merchants who supported the great houses. Moreover, certain streets became the sites of clusters of commercial premises which supplied the needs of the wealthy for luxury goods.[11] Bond Street, which had been the site of hotels and other lodgings for visitors to London, became the centre of sartorial fashion. At the beginning of the nineteenth century all manner of trades concerned with male fashion – including wig makers, tailors and barbers – settled on Bond Street and fed the demand of West End society for elegance and good grooming.[12] These service trades were quite aggressive in their quest for customers and profit, a voracity equalled by those eager to consume their wares.[13] Topography and geography were then indicators of social status and life on the edges of these class-orientated boundaries of the metropolis and can reveal the relationship between the haute bourgeoisie and the petite bourgeoisie. Lower rates of housing and locations that were a little too close to less desirable areas meant lower rents and a different kind of resident. This is picked up on at the end of the period by Dickens in *Nicholas Nickleby* (1839)

Cadogan Place is the one slight bond that joins two great extremes; it is the connecting link between the aristocratic pavements of Belgrave Square and the barbarism of Chelsea. It is in Sloane Street, but not of it. The people in Cadogan Place look down upon Sloane Street, and think Brompton low. They affect fashion too, and wonder where the New Road is. Not that they claim to be on precisely the same footing as the high folks of Belgrave Square and Grosvenor Place, but they stand in reference to them rather than in the light of those illegitimate children of the great who are content to boast about their connexions, although their connexions disavow them. Wearing as much as they can of the airs and semblances of the loftiest rank, the people of Cadogan Place have the realities of the middle station. It is the conductor which communicates to the inhabitants of regions beyond its limit, the shock of pride of birth and rank, which it has not within itself, but derives from a fountain-head beyond.[14]

The Regent's Park offered another kind of marginal existence with a quite different social make-up. The architectural language of Regent Street and the Regent's Park villas and terraces attracted a return to the city, albeit on its edge, by the middle classes who had fled to the suburbs or satellites of London. This was remarked upon by James Elmes in his *Metropolitan Improvements* (1827) where he rebuked some of the architectural impurities but made the observation that

Trim gardens, lawns and shrubs; towering spires, ample domes, banks clothed with flowers, all elegancies of the town, and all the beauties of the country are co-mingled with happy art and blissful union. They surely must all be the abodes of nobles and princes! No, the majority are the retreats of the happy, free-born sons of commerce, of the wealthy commonality who thus enrich and bedeck the heart of their great empire.

The villas in the Regent's Park, of which 56 were planned, were at once a break from past traditions and an important step in the democratization not only of the villa but also of the social make-up of London.[15] The terraces of West London, Bath and Edinburgh were a common feature of the eighteenth-century city and had done much to form the urban streetscape and appeared in grander form on the perimeter of the park. These terraces, although constrained by the same criteria which governed all rate houses in London, appeared from the outside to be one dwelling – a substantial urban palace – as the frontage of the whole row of houses was treated as a single architectural composition. But the Regent's Park project also introduced a new type of housing into London: the urban villa. Only eight of the villas originally planned were built and these stood in private grounds in the Regent's Park. The lack of high walls or boundary fences around these domains meant that they comprised at once part of the whole landscape of the park and appeared to be situated in a large landscaped setting. In this way they were quite distinctive from both the free-standing aristocratic townhouse belonging to peers like the Duke of Devonshire or the Marquis of Hertford, of which there were many scattered across London, and their rural namesakes. The architectural style of the villas represented this in their references to Greek and Roman antiquity. This styling gave these speculatively built villas at once the gloss and authority of a secondary residence designed by an enthusiastic gentleman amateur and the desirability of a modern urban leasehold dwelling. The villa had provided a balanced contrast between the city and retreat and here it was brought into the city, albeit on the perimeter, providing fresh air and a barrier between the Georgian street plan and the fields beyond.[16] By the early nineteenth century the villa, which had been an aristocratic plaything remaining in the family long after the novelty had worn off, became instead a saleable commodity that frequently changed hands.[17] In the original scheme for the Regent's Park the villas were presented as glorified townhouses on the edge of the city with a link via the new Regent's Street to the centre and most importantly the new street gave an axial link with the royal residence, Carlton House. One of the arguments for the construction of Regent Street had been the need to forge an effective connection between the park and the centre of London. The physical distance from Regent's Park to Carlton House may have been little more than a mile but the time taken to travel this without a direct road through the tangled web of garden squares would have rendered the Regent's Park project unworkable. In 1826, shortly after George IV's decision to move to Buckingham Palace was finalised, the much reduced Regent's Park project was pronounced almost complete. The cachet of the dwellings had been adversely affected by this re-orienting of London and, in any case, the take-up of leases had been unsatisfactory.[18] But the park's role as an interface between the country and the city was commented upon by contemporaries:

We have reason to be thankful that the Regent's Park has saved us from worse places in the same quarter; for it is at all events a park, and has trees and grass, and is breathtaking space between town and country. It has prevented Harley and Wimpole Streets from going further; has checked, in the last quarter at least, the monstrous brick cancer that was extending its arms in every direction.[19]

Putting on the style

Just as aspects of the picturesque movement were absorbed into the urban aesthetic of the Royal Parks so the Burkean sublime helped shape urban experience. The anxieties of the modern city promoted responses of both fascination and fear, making the urban environment a kind of uncanny, sublime experience.[20] This kind of response is the result of the relationship of class to urban space. As Anthony Vidler remarks the basis of this anxiety 'was a fundamental insecurity: that of a newly established class, not quite at home in its home'.[21]

These responses to the metropolis found expression not only in the urban plan but also in London's architecture – especially its style. Regent Street and Regent's Park stand distinct from other speculative development not just through their size and scale and their self-consciously defined role in the social engineering of the modern metropolis; they are also distinctive through the attention paid to architectural style. The majority of speculative developments had little in terms of specifications beyond the material, structural and dimensional requirements of the rate system of houses. Here, by contrast, an arbiter of taste in the persona of John Nash was set up to ensure that the correct standard of architecture and appropriate urban aesthetic was achieved. Nash was more directly involved with the design of Regent Street which was under construction well in advance of the Regent's Park villas and terraces. The developer James Burton carried out much of the work for both projects and his changing working relationship to Nash reveals that although Nash supplied fewer designs the emphasis on the aesthetic beauty of the project did not subside. In March 1821 James Burton took up leases on three plots of ground on the east side of the New Street and in April 1822 he erected houses on several parts of the ground in the west side of the New Street between the Quadrant and Oxford Street. In September of the same year Burton erected houses north of Burlington Street. Only a month later he took up a lease on land to build a house and premises on the east side of the street between Chapel Court and the entrance to the King Street Chapel. The designs for these buildings were supplied by Nash and were adhered to more or less by Burton. This is in contrast to the work in the park where there were no predetermined sites for the terraces – it was up to the individual developers to approach the Commissioners of Woods. They in turn consulted Nash who approved, if he did not supply, the design, comprising an outline plan and main elevation. Stipulations about the building quality and maintenance were outlined in the leases including the use of the uniform Bath stone-coloured stucco common to both the terraces and the villas. In 1823 James Burton also built the western half of York Terrace whilst another speculative developer, W. M. Nurse, involved in both the Regent's Park and Regent's Street, constructed the eastern portion. Both builders agreed to adhere strictly to Nash's design in the interests of uniformity and to create an impressive entrance way into the park via York Gate which was situated between the two terraces. This ability to follow instructions when expedient contrasts with the Burtons' treatment of Chester Terrace 1824–5. Here again the plan was Nash's – comprising the longest terrace in the park at 925 feet, screened by 52 columns over which were to be statues on the theme of the British Worthies. Burton deviated from this monumental design which was intended to rival Paris; as Nash commented the terrace 'was nearly as long as the Tuileries'. An acrimonious dispute ensued and the removal of the forward wings, which marred the 'beauty' of the façade and had been added by Burton, was called for by the Commissioners.[22]

Despite his role as a kind of arbiter of taste Nash's own architecture was not without its critics:

> Mr Nash is a better layer out of grounds than architect, and the public have reason to thank him for what he has done for Regent's Park. Our gratitude on that point induces us to say as little as we can of the houses there, with their topolling statues, and other ornamental efforts to escape from the barrack style.[23]

And the designs of the Regent's Park, although nominally approved by Nash, came under continual scrutiny from the Commissioners who held Nash responsible for any slips in aesthetic standards as the park was seen as an essential part of the upgrading of London. James Burton was the first resident in the park, moving into The Holme in 1818. The Commissioners of Woods disliked the design and remarked to Nash:

> In your observation that 'it is to be lamented, for the beauty of the Park, that Mr Burton was *allowed* to build the sort of House he has built', the Board (having recently inspected the Park and the Villa in question) command me to state to you that they entirely concur; but they cannot record this concurrence, without unequivocally stating to you, at the same time, that in their judgment the whole blame of having suffered such a building to be erected, as well as the considerable expense to which it is their further mortification to find, by your Letter, the Crown has been put in planting out the deformities of this building, rest entirely with yourself; The Board consider it to be your special Duty to take care that any Building to be erected in Marylebone Park should be so constructed as not only not to deform but to constitute a real ornament and a substantial and profitable improvement ... of the Crown's Estate.[24]

In this way the re-shaping of the metropolis went beyond a refined urban plan and the deliberate zoning of classes to the creation of a new aesthetic sensory experience of the city. This was essentially classical, drawing on the architecture of ancient Greece and Rome, and it can be argued that this was a natural sequitur to the West End. Here the upmarket district of London was principally domestic and the advantages of Coade Stone[25] and Liardet Stucco[26] had been used to embellish the town houses of the élite with all'antica detailing. But this was a piecemeal upgrading of the London streetscape and was usually on quite a modest scale as Prince Pückler-Muskau remarked:

> very few persons of rank have what we, on the Continent, call a palace in London. Their palaces, their luxury and their grandeur, are to be seen in the country. The Duke of Devonshire is an exception; – his place in town displays great taste and richness, and a numerous collection of works of art.[27]

5.4   View of Carlton Terrace near the York Pillar, London. (The Atheneum Club is on the right.) Winter Fashions for 1837 and 1838. Coloured aquatint

Regent Street and the Regent's Park had a notional stylistic uniformity never before seen in London. The stylistic elements used in the designs signified the authority of antiquity necessary for the establishment of a new social class and gave the grandeur of antiquity to otherwise ordinary urban dwellings. This is seen chiefly in the imaginative treatment of space as well as the applied antiquity of elements like the Palladian temple portico entrance. Cities like other objects and commodities take on a system of meanings relating to religious, aesthetic and social values relevant to their time. The variety of architectural styles seen in the early nineteenth-century metropolis can be seen as a symbol of a distinctive social system and cultural beliefs (Figure 5.4). The growth of consumerism goes some way towards explaining the importance of the quotations of antique architecture as through them it was possible to 'possess' the past. Knowledge and appreciation of the ancient world and its re-appropriation in the Italian Renaissance was generally enhanced in the opening years of the nineteenth century through increased travel and the proliferation of printed material and the growing collections, both public and private, of artifacts.[28] The philosophy of association also continued to play an important part in the appreciation of antiquity.[29] As

Henry Home, Lord Kames had suggested, architecture could transmit the feeling of grandeur through association with antiquity which helped to engender a feeling of a connection and similarity between the past and the new era in British history. The connection between architecture and urban experience was then the result of an invented memory.[30] The modern metropolis was not merely trying to imitate or copy the ancient world, rather the aesthetic vocabulary of antiquity was appropriated and a new syntax formulated to create an effective national visual language with encoded meanings for the educated classes. This stylistic tradition had been established in the eighteenth century particularly with regard to country house design.[31] It was now brought into the city where it represented and was reinforced by the urban bourgeoisie and the kind of cultural imperialism displayed in the huge collections of Greco Roman antiquities being amassed and displayed in the capital.[32]

New society new sobriety

Richard Dighton's two volumes entitled *City Characters* and *West End Characters* (1825) pinpointed many of the social divisions between the two areas of London. Dighton concentrates on dress, specifically male fashion, as a means of highlighting the functional businesslike character of the City merchant or trader and the 'must have' mannered elegance of the independently wealthy and socially connected West End dandy. At the beginning of the nineteenth century the dandy carried on the tradition of his eighteenth-century counterpart who was known as 'macaroni' and was often caricatured in prints and parodied in novels. The dandy did not disappear from social view until the 1840s and he was without doubt a kind of flâneur. The importance of the rituals of social dress code to the early nineteenth-century young man about town reveals how this manifestation of style represented the intricate system of social hierarchy to become a kind of tribal marking. Prince Pückler-Muskau noted this in a letter of 1827 where he reports on the remarks of his washerwoman who found herself in great demand by the fashionable élite:

[she] is the only person who can make cravats of the right stiffness, or fold the breasts of shirts with plaits of the right size. An 'élégant' [dandy], then, requires per week – twenty shirts; twenty-four pocket handkerchiefs; nine or ten pairs of 'summer trousers'; thirty neck handkerchiefs (unless he wears black ones); a dozen waistcoats; and stockings … a dandy cannot get on without dressing three or four times a day, the affair is 'tout simple', for he must appear: 1st. Breakfast toilette, – a chintz dressing gown and Turkish slippers; 2nd. Morning riding dress – a frock coat, boots and spurs; 3rd. Dinner dress – dress coat and shoes; 4th. ball dress, with 'pumps', a word signifying shoes as thin as paper.[33]

The early nineteenth-century dandy socialised with his peers in the dining clubs and coffee houses of the West End. These were the preserve of the socially well connected and membership was often determined on political beliefs. Those of Whig sympathies had traditionally been members of Brook's whilst Tories had joined White's. But as Percy's *History* noted the political affiliations of these clubs were giving way in the face of the new arrivals which represented a broader social spectrum and a more varied range of interests and activities: 'As party names are rapidly passing into oblivion it is very probable, ere long, that the political distinctions of these two club houses will cease'.[34]

The emergence of the purpose built club house which gave a public face to these institutions raised important questions about the stylistic language of design. One of the earliest examples of these new institutions was the Athenaeum founded in 1824 by the MP John Wilson Croker as a club for 'Literary and Scientific men and followers of the Fine Arts'. Despite its name and high aspirations the membership was not restricted to the titled or very wealthy and included the architect of the club's new premises Decimus Burton, Sir Humphry Davy, Sir Francis Chantrey and Sir Robert Smirke with Michael Faraday as its first secretary. The Athenaeum was begun in 1827 on part of the site where Carlton House Palace had stood until its demolition in the preceding year (Figure 5.4). As its name implies it was styled in the Grecian manner which was the height of fashion. It is tempting to suggest that the style reflected the architect's and the members' vision of London as the new Athens and was a monument to the new society. But the Athenaeum signified a far more complex reading of the social landscape of London. The other half of the site which straddled the southern end of Regent Street was occupied by the United Service Club which catered for both the Army and the Navy. The architect for these premises was John Nash who was also in charge of all matters of architectural style for the New Street. Whereas Burton's design could be read as being in sympathy with the aims of the Athenaeum this reading is called into question as Burton was held in check by Nash, who insisted on complete stylistic uniformity between the two club houses and that Burton's design should follow his.[35] The lengthy dialogue between the two architects and Burton's frustration at Nash's tardiness and indecision is not the subject here. What is important is that the styling of these two important buildings in the urban streetscape is considered in terms of its contribution to the metropolitan aesthetic rather than being representative of the ideology of the two institutions. On another level it is tempting to read the siting of these clubs for the new society on the site of the opulently decorated but ultimately inadequate home of the king as a symbol of the new middle-class sobriety. But they were also, like Carlton House, set pieces in the new metropolitan plan.

5.5   The Club Houses etc., Pall Mall, (Reform Club in centre), 1842. Coloured tinted lithograph

The growth of London's clubland, which was centred along Pall Mall in the period 1800–1840, maps out the changing nature of London society and the growth of the metropolis as a focus for social activity and a new kind of public existence (Figure 5.5). The drinking, gambling and other sybaritic pleasure that had characterised the eighteenth-century forerunners of the new London clubs gave way to a more serious outlook. The new society with its new sobriety wanted calm, reading rooms, libraries and intelligent debate with like-minded souls. Prince Pückler-Muskau, perhaps from the vantage point of a foreign visitor, made some acute observation on London's clubland:

In the absence of society, the various Clubs, (to which, in contrary to former custom, a stranger can now gain admittance,) are a very agreeable resource. Our ambassador introduced me into two of them, – the United Service Club, into which no foreigners are admitted except ambassadors and military men, – the latter the rank of staff officers: and the Travellers' Club, into which every foreigner of education, who has good introductions is admitted. ... In Germany [Muskau's own country], people have as little notion of the elegance and comfort of Clubs, as of the rigorous execution of their laws which prevail here.
All that luxury and convenience, without magnificence, demand, is here to be found in as great perfection as in the best private houses. ... In the elegant well-furnished library there is also a person always at hand to fetch the books you want.[36]

The engaging of the innovative chef Soyer at the Reform Club ensured the reputation of London's clubland as the sybaritic sublime. Puckler-Muskau had already identified this trend:

The table, – I mean eating, – with most men the first thing, and with me not the last, – is generally prepared by a French cook, as well and as cheaply as it is possible to have it in London. As the Club provides the wines [which are] very drinkable.[37]

The German prince, perhaps inadvertently, noted the consequence of all this indulgence: 'Even scales, by which to ascertain one's weight daily – a strange taste of the English' were to be found in the well-furnished London clubs.[38]

The Travellers' Club, founded in 1819, aimed 'to form a point of reunion for gentleman who had travelled to abroad'. But this went beyond the dilettanti image of the Grand Tour to represent a serious engagement with the foreign as seen in its founding members. Lords Palmerston and Castlereagh were both concerned with foreign policy whereas the architect C. R. Cockerell and the collector and dealer in antiquities W. R. Hamilton were concerned with a detailed mapping and amassing of knowledge of foreign artifacts. The former revived the building styles of the ancients in his design whilst the latter was closely involved with the shipping of the Elgin Marbles. The club house adjacent to the Athenaeum was designed by Charles Barry in 1829 and resembled an Italian Renaissance palazzo. Are we to read this as the middle classes representing themselves as the new Florentine merchants – patrons of the Renaissance? The Reform Club might reinforce this argument. The Westminster Reform Club enjoyed greater tolerance after the 1832 Reform Bill and in 1837 acquired land next to the Travellers' Club on Pall Mall. Barry was again the architect and he produced an opulent Italian Renaissance palazzo design which was one storey higher than its neighbours. This provided accommodation for the members.[39] But if London's clubland was a haven for the new society and represented the rising political importance of the middle class it becomes harder to explain the choice of a gothic style, albeit set within a classical meter, for the new Palace of Westminster. The Houses of Parliament were rebuilt after the 1832 Reform Act and expressed a new national identity. But the idea of a gothic club house or a gothic West End presents an uncanny image of a society that is not 'at home in its home'. These signifiers of the pre-eminence of certain social groups relied on the architectural vocabulary and syntax of the ancient world as they represented the petite bourgeoisie's emulation of the grande bourgeoisie. The new Houses of Parliament marked a break with this practice by refocusing on indigenous architectural traditions in the construction of national identities. But in both cases the various masks of the past were necessary to settle the class-based social anxieties of the present.

Public life

The increasing importance of London as the central hub of the social, economic and political life of the nation resulted in a more exposed public life
for those involved in these spheres. And it is here that the two realms of
aristocratic élite and the bourgeoisie run parallel, showing at once the static
nature of social life and the process of adaptation necessary for the inclusion
of the expanding middle class. These kinds of rigid social structure are often
seen most clearly from the outside and here Prince Pückler-Muskau again
offers a insight into the long-standing hierarchical nature of English society:

> In the relations and tone of society, on the one hand, from the highest step to the
> very lowest, not a trace of any element of republicanism is to be found. Here,
> everything is in the highest degree ultra aristocratic – it is caste like.

That said he notes the rather subdued role of the monarchy:

> The Kings of England live like private men; most of the high officers about the court
> are little more than nominal and are seldom assembled except on occasions of great
> ceremony. Now as somewhere in society as a focus must be organised, from which
> the highest light and the highest authority in all matters connected with society
> must emanate, the rich aristocracy seem here called to assume this station.[40]

But public life had its limits as the season ruled city life. Throughout the early
part of the nineteenth century, however, the season became longer and longer
as parliamentary sessions and the volume of business increased and those
participating in government were less concerned with their country estates if
they had one.[41] Moreover the metropolis had become the hub of the nation. It
was at once a centre of commerce and fashion and typified the very life force
of the nation. Nevertheless, the enduring tradition of spending time away
from town impacted on social life as theatres and other places of public
entertainments followed the habits of the élite and closed out of season.

> London is deserted by the fashionables; and that with such affectation, that many
> who are obliged to remain on business positively conceal themselves. The streets in
> the west end of the town are like those of a deserted city.[42]

During the season social life in the metropolis was busy if not vigorous. The
royal court was the apogee of social interchange and offered the élite the
opportunity to perform the kinds of rituals which defined their caste:

> I am just back from the Levée, which was very numerously attended. The King was
> obliged to sit, on account of his gout, but looked very well. The Duke of Wellington
> returned thanks for his elevation to the Premiership by falling on both knees,
> whereas it is usual only to kneel on one. His gratitude was probably double, on
> account of his double quality of Prime Minister and former Commander-in-Chief. ...
> almost everyone is admitted to these levées if they can but appear in the prescribed
> dress.[43]

5.6   Regent Street, looking towards the Duke of York's Column, 1842. Lithograph

Yet it was the party circuit which provided the most active social life and it was not unusual to attend several balls in one evening.

A curious foreigner who wishes to see all gradations of social life, can hardly hold out a London season. More than forty invitations are now lying on my table, – five or six for each day.[44]

Many of the social rituals and cultural practices of the ruling élite took place behind closed doors in private residences. Whereas the Royal Parks and other urban open spaces provided outdoor sites of social interchange there were few respectable indoor places for such spontaneous activity for the upper and middle classes. Despite the enthusiasm for good food, as seen in London's clubland, there were few public restaurants and the best of these were foreign. For instance Sablonière's in Leicester Square was established in 1788 followed by Bertolini's in St Martin's Street. Unlike other European cities there was no café society with establishments like Verrey's in Regent Street being 'one of the nearest imitations to a café to be found in the metropolis' (Figure 5.6).[45]

The resistance to public life by the middle class was part of the wish for segregation and privacy.[46] Most public places, especially public houses, failed to accommodate these changes and offered little in the way of spatial differentiation between classes in their internal arrangement. The coffee house, which had been a feature of metropolitan life since the late seventeenth century remained a popular meeting place and its system of discrete booths or boxes where strangers and friends would sit together and converse encouraged an acceptable form of social heterogeneity. But these remained male-dominated spaces. Unsurprisingly a double standard existed in attitudes towards the appearance and behaviour of men and women in public places. It was feared that women might be educated or toughened through contact with urban life and the inevitable outcome of this for them, unlike men, would be disgrace. Some coffee houses had spaces set apart where men could take their wives and daughters, although women could not go there unaccompanied as their presence would have been considered 'fast, if not disreputable'. For the most part unaccompanied women who wished to dine were confined to pastry or confectioner's shops as described by Dickens in *Dombey and Son* (1846–8) where Miss Tox sought refuge 'in a musty little back room usually devoted to the consumption of soups, and pervaded by an ox-tail atmosphere'. The only respite from this repressive social regime was the shopping arcade or shopping street. It was remarked later in the century that here 'ladies can conveniently lunch when in town for a day's shopping and unattended by a gentleman'.[47] And as early as 1815 *The Epicure's Almanack* recorded several such establishments in the West End including Farrance's in Spring Gardens and Owen and Bentley's fruit shop in New Bond Street, noted for its jellies, ices and liquors.[48] Despite these specific sites women remained largely on the edge of this kind of public life. But as the metropolis became a more self-consciously constructed artefact and through this a physical and mental 'home' for the bourgeoisie, the notions of class, consumption, display and gender became ever more public.

Notes

1. See T. Veblen, *The Theory of the Leisure Class*, 1899.

2. T. Adorno, 'Veblen's Attack on Culture', *Prisms*, London, Spearman, 1967.

3. S. and R. Percy, *The Percy History and Interesting memorial on the rise, progress and present state of all the capitals of Europe*, 3 vols, London, 1823, III, 355.

4. For an account of the development of Regent's Park see A. Saunders, *Regent's Park from 1086 to the Present Day*, London, Bedford College, London, 1981.

5. Report from the Select Committee on the Office of Works, 1828, 74.

6. Ibid.

7. As a result of complaints from the residents of Piccadilly and St James's that it was a nuisance, Haymarket was moved to Cumberland Market, Regent's Park.

8. 53 Geo. III, c. 121. For a discussion of the prominence of slaughter houses and animal remains on the London streets see D. Donald, 'Beastly Sights: the treatment of animals as a moral theme in representations of London' in D. Arnold (ed.) *The Metropolis and its Image: constructing identities for London c 1750–1950*, Oxford, The Association of Art Historians and Blackwell, 1999, 48–78.

9. Report from the Committee on the Petition of the Tradesmen and Inhabitants of Norris Street and Market Terrace, 1817 (79) iii. 83.

10. PRO Cres 26/188.

11. On this point see R. Walker, *The Savile Row Story*, London, Prior, 1988.

12. For a fuller discussion see A. Ribeiro, *Dress and Morality*, New York, Holmes and Meier, 1986, 111–14 esp.

13. The Berners Street Hoax of 1809 typifies the prolific production and consumption of goods where in pursuit of winning a wager Theodore Hook ordered all manner of tradespeople and merchants to the modest house of a widow, Mrs Tottenham, at the same time. See F. Barker and P. Jackson, *London 200 Years of a City and its People*, London, Cassell, 1974, 248.

14. Charles Dickens, *Nicholas Nickleby*, 1839, 339.

15. For a full discussion of the Regent's Park villas see my essay 'A Family Affair: Decimus Burton's villa designs for the Regent's Park' in D. Arnold (ed.) *The Georgian Villa*, Stroud and New York, Sutton Publishing, 1998, 105–17.

16. The concept of the villa is discussed in my introduction to *The Georgian Villa*, *op. cit.*, ix–xii.

17. The residents of the park are discussed in *The Villas in Regent's Park and their Residents*, The Marylebone Society, London, 1959.

18. See my essay 'A Family Affair: Decimus Burton's villa designs for the Regent's Park' *op. cit.*

19. Leigh Hunt 'The Townsman' nos 2, 3 and 4 reprinted in *Political and Occasional Essays*, ed. L. and C. Houchans, New York, Columbia University Press, 1962, 289–90.

20. On this point see A. Vidler, *The Architectural Uncanny: Essays in the modern unhomely*, Cambridge, Mass., MIT, 1992, 3 esp.

21. Ibid., 3–4.

22. William Wilkins was brought in to settle any compensation payable by the Crown. In a private letter to Alexander Milne dated 6 May 1826 Nash stated his opinion about the dispute:

    It is very painful circumstance to oppose or appear to oppose Mr Burton for whom I entertain considerable regard – but I feel that I ought not to stand by and see the Commissioners enter into a partial enquiry in which loss is assumed on one side without taking into consideration advantages which that side desire from a departure from their engagement, or from disposing of the ground in a manner unauthorized by that engagement – I feel this sentiment still more strongly from entertaining a different opinion as to the necessity of taking down the Houses, convinced that the removal of them will produce a worse effect than by altering the screen so as to obscure the buildings which are behind.

23. Leigh Hunt *op. cit.*, 289–90.

24. Letter from Alexander Milne, Secretary to the Commissioners of the Office of Woods and Forests, to John Nash.

25. For a full account of the development and use of Coade Stone see A. Kelly, *Mrs Coade and her Stone*, Upton upon Severn, Self Publishing Association in conjunction with The Georgian Group, 1990.

26. The development of Liardet Stucco and its use by Robert Adam in his speculative developments is discussed in F. Kelsall, 'Liardet Stucco', *Architectural History*, 27, 1984.

27. E. M. Butler (ed.) *A Regency Visitor, The English Tour of Prince Pückler-Muskau Described in his letters 1826–1828*, Collins, London, 1957, letter dated 25 March 1827, 180–1.

28. For a discussion of the role of the Townley Marbles in the formation of the British Museum see D. Cook, 'The Townley Marbles in Westminster and Bloomsbury', The British Museum Yearbook, 2, 1977, BM Publications, London.

29. Key texts which developed and refined these ideas include Addison's *The Pleasures of the Imagination*, 1712; Edmund Burke's *Philosophical Enquiry into the Origin of our Idea of the Sublime and the Beautiful*, 1757; and Kames' *Elements of Criticism*, 1785. For a discussion of the philosophy of association and its relationship to architectural aesthetics see D. Watkin, 'Sir John Soane and the Philosophy of Association' in D. Arnold (ed.) *The Picturesque in late Georgian England*, London, The Georgian Group, 1995.

30. On this point see S. Freud, 'Civilization and its Discontents' in *Civilization, Society and Religion*, Penguin Freud Library, 12, ed. A. Dickson, Harmondsworth, Penguin, 1991, 251–340.

31. On this point see my chapter 'The Illusion of Grandeur?: antiquity, Grand Tourism and the country house', in *The Georgian Country House: architecture, landscape and society*, Stroud and New York, Sutton Publishing, 1998, 100–16

32. On the growth of these collections and their meaning see *inter alia* I. Jenkins, 'Athens Rising Near the Pole: London, Athens and the idea of freedom', in C. Fox (ed.) *London World City*, London and New Haven, Yale University Press, 1992, 143–54.

33. E. M. Butler *op. cit.*, letter dated 8 July 1828, 332–3.

34. S. and R. Percy *op. cit.*, I, 13.

35. The evolution of the designs and the relationship between the two architects is documented in PRO Cres 2/710 and PRO Cres 2/711.

36. E. M. Butler *op. cit.*, letter dated 20 November 1826, 70–72.

37. Ibid., 72.

38. Ibid., 70.

39. The Athenaeum responded to this by adding an attic storey designed by Decimus Burton in 1858.

40. E. M. Butler *op. cit.*, letter dated 8 July 1828, 332–3.

41. On this point see M. H. Port, 'Town House Country House: their interaction', in D. Arnold, *The Georgian Country House: architecture, landscape and society, op. cit.*, 117–38.

42. E. M. Butler *op. cit.*, letter dated 15 August 1827, 246.

43. Ibid., letter dated 27 March 1828, 308.

44. Ibid., letter dated 22 April 1827, 206

45. E. H. Malcolm, 'London Coffee Houses and their Customers', *Tegg's Magazine*, 1, 1844, 124.

46. The question of public life is discussed in a European context in R. Sennett, *The Fall of Public Man*, Cambridge, Cambridge University Press, 1977.

47. *Women's Gazette*, 1, August 1876, 174.

48. *The Epicure's Almanack or Calendar of Good Living*, London, Longmans, 1815, 133.

6

To Gaze, to Admire, and to Covet

The thematic exploration of the metropolis as a site of display embraces at once its architecture, topographies and collections, which are all fundamental aspects of the urban environment. But these elements are in turn signifiers of different sets of cultural meanings and values which are themselves open to interpretation. On one level the city can be seen as a repository for a variety of cultural artifacts or indeed an object in its own right. But if we accept that any kind of artistic production has different meanings we can read the relationship of the early nineteenth-century metropolis to both visual and material culture in several ways. These relate specifically to the social and cultural meaning of the architecture, collections and urban land-scapes, and following on from this the way in which these elements were consumed by a range of publics. After all, something can only be displayed if it is to be viewed. But beyond this the city gave a physical location to the social rituals and cultural practices which were hallmarks of polite society in the opening years of the nineteenth century – and these were as much part of the notion of display as any artefact. In this way the metropolis functioned as a spectacle of its different constituencies.

The period of colonisation and economic expansion in the eighteenth and early nineteenth centuries also saw the continuation of the nation's belief in its cultural superiority over the rest of Europe, if not the world. Commensurate with this was a changing attitude towards commodities which reflected movements in the social order and the steady growth of a consumer society during the period.[1] For those who undertook the Grand Tour this desire for ownership was satisfied both by the cultural appreciation of the sights of Europe and by the availability of objects for purchase. Remnants of antiquity whether they be sculptures, architectural fragments or quotations of antique architecture became part of a currency of material culture disembodied from their original context but with related sets of meanings. This touristic appreciation and absorbtion of another culture, whether past or present, relied on the collection or memory of a set of displaced forms which are elements dislodged from their original historical cultural contexts. In the early nineteenth-century metropolis the rise of public and private collections with some edifying potential established a new kind of interface with the past which relied less on wealth as a means of travel. And in turn these objects served to construct a social identity. The importance of the emergent consumer society and with it the emphasis on material culture is an essential element in understanding the relationship between antiquity and the city as site of display. This was a defining moment in the way in which possessions were used to embellish social status and represent taste. The opening decades of the nineteenth century witnessed not only tightening systems of ordering knowledge of the past but also a shift in attitudes towards modern manufactures and technology, which also became indicators of rank. Objects and commodities take on a system of meanings relating to social and cultural values of their time. It is easy to see how collectibles displayed with such pride were seen as symbols of a distinctive social system and cultural beliefs. This fetishisation of the object tells us even more about their meaning in the increasingly democratised urban consumer society of the early nineteenth century.

Architecture and the display of private collections

The self-conscious production of an *all'antica* architectural aesthetic and the amassing of collections of antiquities were indicators of taste, wealth and status. A re-reading of these aspects of the city reveals perhaps more similarities than differences between them particularly with reference to the notion of display. The re-use and citation of antique architectural forms has already been shown to parallel in many ways the culture of collecting.[2] Here the external or alien elements of Greco Roman art, architecture and aesthetic ideals were adopted as signifiers of a distinct set of social and cultural values and absorbed into the British aesthetic repertoire. But the city's role as a site of display extends from the quotations of all'antica elements in its architecture and decoration to a more metaphorical display of a unique and self-consciously defined social and intellectual culture as well as its function as a repository for artifacts. The collections held in public institutions and private townhouses are testament to the enthusiasm and purchasing power of travellers and the emerging urban intelligentsia. Whole houses like Hertford House or Thomas Hope's Duchess Street Mansion became sites of display. Visiting and consuming sights and sites of cultural value and the display of the material culture of past societies in public galleries and private houses

6.1   Decimus Burton, The Grove, Regent's Park, 1822. Watercolour

was one way of subordinating these into an established set of values and ideologies belonging to a modern British identity. As the passion for the consumption and display of collections grew, new structures and additions to existing buildings, became necessary so changing the architectural face of the city.

The Regent's Park villas were potent symbols of the new kind of metropolitan society. They functioned as signifiers of wealth, status and social aspiration through their setting, which gave the appearance of a residence which stood alone in the park, the all'antica architectural styling and the objects displayed in their principal rooms. Two of the eight villas constructed offer examples of the juxtaposition of different social cultures in London in the opening years of the nineteenth century. The Grove (1822) was designed by Decimus Burton for his friend George Bellas Greenough, a natural scientist. The house has a compact plan and cites elements of the Erechtheum on the Acropolis in Athens in its architectural styling (Figure 6.1).[3] The Grecian theme is continued inside the villa where over the bookcases dividing the two libraries was a plaster frieze cast of the Panathenaic procession from the Parthenon.[4] Greenough's collection of specimens relating to the natural world were housed in purpose-designed mahogany cabinets. The villa was at once a home, a workplace and a symbol of the increased interest in the amassing and ordering of knowledge of the known world.

6.2   Decimus Burton, south façade of St Dunstan's Villa, Regent's Park, home of
Marquis of Hertford, 1825

St Dunstan's, designed by Decimus Burton for the Marquis of Hertford,
offers a complete contrast to the sobriety, neatness and intellectual integrity
of the design for the Grove (Figure 6.2).[5] The villa was situated in the northwest corner of the park with the garden façade overlooking the serpentine
lake rather like the Grove and the Holme. The occupant was a colourful
figure who was the basis of the Marquis of Steyne in Thackeray's *Vanity Fair*
and Disraeli's Marquis of Monmouth in *Coningsby*. Designs for the Marquis
of Hertford's villa were exhibited at the Royal Academy in 1822 and the villa
completed by 1825.[6] It became known as St Dunstan's Villa as the clock of
Old St Dunstan's in the West was purchased by the Marquis and sited in the
grounds from 1832 onwards. The Marquis already owned Hertford House, a
first-rate 'private palace' with an outstanding collection of fine and decorative art. His villa was an additional residence designed principally for
entertaining. The plan allows the best possible space for entertainment and
provides a continuous enfilade of rooms of varying sizes and dimensions,
each offering the possibility of different types of entertainment and the
pursuit of other sybaritic pleasures as well as a splendid array of objects. The
singer Carl Maria von Weber vividly recounts the scene and the fate of both
himself and the opera company which had been engaged to entertain the
guests at one of the regular vast assemblies hosted by the Marquis at his
urban villa:

A magnificent room, 500–600 people there, all of the greatest brilliance. … The shrieking and jabbering of this throng of humanity was quite atrocious. While I played they tried to get a little quiet. … But what can they have heard. … Meanwhile I thought hard about my thirty guineas. … At last, about 2 o'clock, they went into supper, whereupon I took my leave.

The splendour of Hertford's London houses did, however, impress his guests and this opulence is ably articulated by Prince Pückler-Muskau:

In the evening a great fete at Lord Hertford's, with concert, ball, French play etc., assembled the fashionable and half-fashionable world in a magnificent and tastefully furnished house. The singularity in it is, that all the rooms are decorated in the same manner, – flesh-coloured stucco and gold, with black bronze, very large looking glasses, and curtains of crimson and white silk. This uniformity produces as very 'grandiose' effect. One room alone (of extraordinary size for London) is white and gold, carpeted with scarlet cloth, and with furniture and curtains of the same colour.[7]

Lord Hertford's London villa and townhouse in Manchester Square provide excellent examples of the magnificence of the 'private palaces' of some members of the aristocracy which equalled if not eclipsed their country seats. For instance, Devonshire House on Piccadilly was the more than adequate urban counterpart of Chatsworth in Derbyshire.[8] The sums spent on grand refurbishment schemes by the Earl of Grosvenor in 1808 and the 6th Duke of Devonshire in 1811 ran into tens of thousands of pounds, whilst the Duke of Northumberland established himself as the most serious rival to the extravagant George IV when he spent upwards of £150,000 on the refurbishment of his townhouse in 1820. The developing importance of the townhouse in terms of its form and function can be mapped against the increasing importance of London as a nexus of social and political systems.[9] As such these metropolitan dwellings functioned like their country counterparts as symbols of the ruling élite where the status and breeding of the occupiers of town houses was evident in their innate 'taste'. But unlike their rural cousins these urban palaces were usually only on show to their occupants' social equals. Some private collections did, however, carry with them the notion of public edification – as well as signifying the status of the owner. Charles Townley's (1737–1805) collection of sculptures, medals and gems was probably the best known private collection in London in the late eighteenth century and was displayed in Townley's house, 7 Park Street (now Queen Anne's Gate), where visitors of the right social class and of genuine interest were allowed to visit and study it. There was a printed catalogue and watercolour images of the interior show how the collection was displayed – the most important sculptures being in the dining room.[10] Townley preferred to display his prestigious collection in his London home than at his country house in Lancashire as it reached a wider public and was therefore a more effective signifier of his status and taste. The idea of the townhouse as a kind

6.3   Thomas Hope, Third Vase Room, Duchess Street Mansion, c 1800

of personal museum was taken up and developed by the Dutch emigré Thomas Hope who embraced the notion of the display of personal posses- sions as a signifier of rank if not the practice of self-creation. Hope's Duchess Street mansion presented an ordered experience of the occupant's extensive collection of Greco Roman artifacts and furniture made to his own designs. Each room had a distinct theme and signalled the kind of taxonomic ar- rangement that was to become a feature of public collections (Figure 6.3). But Hope's house and collection were not without their critics.[11] Prince Pückler-Muskau disliked Hope's Duchess Street mansion and his furniture designs and made some disparaging remarks in his letters:

Mr Hope ... appeared to me no ordinary man. He is very rich, and his house is full of treasures of art, and of luxuries which I shall describe hereafter. His furniture theory, which is fashioned on the antique, I cannot praise in practice:– the chairs are ungovernable; other trophy-like structures look ridiculous, and the sophas have sharp salient points in all directions, that an incautious sitter might hurt himself seriously.[12]

Private houses could then be sites of display for those of a certain social caste. But the emergence of the architect as a cultured individual rather than craftsman in the opening years of the nineteenth century brought with it a new kind of collection and methods of display. Casts and fragments of antique sculpture and architectural detail had long been part of the collec- tion of a connoisseur. But in the offices of professional architects these artifacts provided practising designers, together with their pupils and their clients, a visual encyclopedia of references to the visual culture of the past. Moreover, the amassing and display of these objects enhanced the status of the architect both socially and intellectually. Three of the leading architects in early nineteenth-century Britain had comprehensive collections of antiquities, casts and fine art. The way in which each collection was used and displayed reveals how objects were used to embellish social reputation and the importance of re-appropriated artifacts in the processes of design.

Sir John Soane's house and office on Lincoln's Inn Fields (1812–13) was one of the best known sights of the metropolis and it appeared in many guidebooks. The architect's dwelling housed his ever-expanding collection of architectural sculpture details, sculptures and drawings. The eclectic, unordered display of these artifacts was testament to the breadth of the collection but also to its function as an educative tool. Here architect and pupils encountered the jumble that was Rome and experienced at first hand whole and fragmented objects whether original or cast. But the important thing was that this collection remained in the public domain and that it was used as part of the formative process of architectural production.[13] This democratised the public's engagement with the antique in the same way as the display of the artifacts of ancient Greece and Rome in the British Museum. Soane did not however miss the opportunity to embellish his own reputation and enhance his social status through his collection. The artist B. R. Haydon gives a glimpse of the experience the beau monde who gathered at the house in Lincoln's Inn Fields in 1825 at Soane's invitation to gaze upon (if not admire and covet) the newly arrived ancient Egyptian Sarcophagus of Seti.

I was at Soane's last night to see his sarcophagus by lamplight … [the house] is a perfect Cretan labyrinth: curious narrow staircases, landing places, balconies, spring doors, and little rooms filled with fragments to the very ceiling. It was the finest fun imaginable to see people come into the library after wandering about below, amidst tombs and capitals, and shafts, and noseless heads, with an expression of delighted relief at finding themselves again among the living, and with coffee and cake! They looked as if they were pleased to feel their blood circulate once more, and went smirking up to Soane, *lui faisant leur compliments,* with a twisting chuckle of features as if grateful for their escape. Fancy delicate ladies of fashion dipping their pretty heads into an old mouldy, fusty, hieroglyphicked coffin, blessing their stars at its age, wondering whom it contained. … The Duke of Sussex … putting his royal head into the coffin, added his wonder to the wonder of the rest.

Soane remained upstairs throughout the soirée 'smiling and flushed by flattery' enjoying the compliments paid to him, his collection and his generosity in opening it to polite society whilst, according to Haydon, remaining unaware of the comments being made out of his earshot that his house was 'funny' and 'curious'. But despite the judgemental comments of Soane's guests, Haydon estimated that

There was not a soul then around him [Soane] who would not, ere they put on their night-caps, envy him his assemblage of rank and talent and fashion; sneer at his antiques, quiz his coffee, and go to sleep, pitying with affected superiority his delusion and vanity.[14]

The display of collections as a means of social advancement did not escape the notice of John Nash, the favoured architect of George IV. Nash, together with Sir Robert Smirke, was one of Soane's fellow attached architects to the Office of Works. He was responsible for the laying out of Regent Street where he built two houses nos 14 and 16 between 1819–23 for himself and his cousin Mr Edwards. The layout of the houses interlocked as they had no party wall, Nash's accommodation was mostly on the principal floor and this allowed him to build an elegant suite of rooms. Nash had a substantial collection of casts but they were displayed in a completely different fashion from that used by Soane. The casts were part of a large collection of art objects including copies of old master paintings and fine furniture which were displayed in 'showroom style', rather than in any didactic fashion, in Nash's London house.[15] Of particular note is the seventy-foot long gallery which was luxuriously decorated and presented an array of casts of classical sculptures, paintings and architectural details.[16] The interiors of this splendid townhouse made a considerable impression on its visitors. Of note here is the response of Prince Pückler-Muskau, perhaps one of the most experienced visitors to the houses of the élite in early nineteenth-century Britain who remarked

I have paid several visits to Mr Nash, to whom I am indebted for much valuable instruction in my art. He is said to have 'erected' an enormous fortune. He has a beautiful country house, and no artist is more handsomely lodged in town. I was particularly pleased with his library. It consists of a long and wide gallery, with twelve deep niches on each side, and two large doorways at the ends, leading into two other spacious rooms. In each niche is a semi-circular window in the roof and on the wall a fresco painting, copied from the 'Logge di Rafaelle'; and below these, casts of the best antique statues, on pedestals. The remaining space in the niches is occupied by books, which however, rise no higher than the pedestal of the statues. Arabesques also copied from those of the Vatican, admirably executed in fresco, adorn the broad pilasters between the niches.
  All the space on the walls or pilasters not covered with paintings is of pale red stucco, with small gold mouldings. The execution seems thoroughly finished and excellent.[17]

There is no doubt that Nash's social ambition was greater than Soane's, although a knighthood eluded him. These aspirations manifested themselves in the display of Nash's extensive collection in his Regent Street house which echoed those of the aristocratic interiors of the 'private palaces'.

The most enigmatic of these architects' houses was that occupied by Decimus Burton, architect to the Office of Woods, in Spring Gardens from

1827. Little is known except that the architect's house had a 'Grecian Room'[18] and this presumably housed Burton's extensive collection of over 226 casts he had purchased en bloc in November 1827.[19] Burton's own inventory of the casts, which appears in Appendix 1, shows that the range of casts and the buildings from which architectural details were taken conform to the standard pattern of study after antique and other Roman buildings undertaken by Grand Tourists, so implying that this was a purchase of a coherent collection. As Burton did not go on a Grand Tour, his casts may well have formed part of his continuing training as well as being an educative tool for his pupils' use. The only visual evidence of the interior of Spring Gardens is a small undated watercolour.[20] It is identified on the reverse, in Burton's hand, as 'Spring Gardens lobby at the top of the stairs looking from the dining room' (Figure 6.4). This possibly shows the huge capital of the Temple of Vesta at Tivoli surrounded by unidentified smaller pieces which greeted the visitor as s/he ascends the stairs. This may well be the entrance to the Grecian Room a kind of annex to the house where Burton displayed his collection which, as his catalogue suggests, was hung in some kind of didactic order.[21] The house in Spring Gardens, unlike its counterparts on Regent Street and Lincoln's Inn Fields goes unmentioned in contemporary commentaries. But the absence of a public face for this extensive collection serves only to emphasize how the possession and display of artifacts from the ancient world was an essential part of the construction of a social identity – no matter how private this was.

The viewing public remained largely at a distance from the private collections and splendid interiors in the metropolis as the town houses of the aristocracy did not have an open door policy, although those with a genuine interest in the collections were able to view the interiors of the dwellings of Townley and Hope. Architect's houses catered for a different but no less important constituency of the populace but the number of visitors remained small. These facets of the nature of domestic display do however reinforce the role of the townhouse as a signifier of taste and status which filtered through into the urban consciousness of the middle classes. Moreover, the luxury trades supported and developed by grand refurbishment schemes such as those carried out on the 'private palaces' ensured both a buoyant market and the production of less expensive modern manufactures for those who wished to follow the lead of the upper echelons of society. Many of these goods drew inspiration for their design from antiquity whilst embracing the potential of modern technology in their production and function. These consumables helped create a spectacle of luxury, wealth and cultural hegemony across the tradesmen's showrooms of the metropolis.

6.4   Decimus Burton, Spring Gardens Lobby at the top of the stairs looking from the Dining Room, undated

A nation of shopkeepers

London was crucial for the growing world commodity market and was the largest manufacturing centre in Britain. As metropolitan society grew in size, importance and wealth so the showrooms of provincial manufacturers were established in the capital to meet the ever increasing demand. As William Darton recorded 'Most of the great streets appropriated to shops have an unrivalled aspect of wealth and splendour; ... manufactures form the chief ornament'.[22] The influx of luxury goods into the showrooms of London became one of the sights of the city:

here you discover wealth and magnificence that you would look in vain elsewhere for ... . It is important not to be astonished at seeing this riches displayed. Here the costly shawls from the East Indies ... silk-tissues from China ... home manufactures of the most exquisite taste, an ocean of rings, watches, chains, bracelets, and aigrettes, ready-dresses, ribbons, lace, bonnets ... attract, tempt and astonish your eyes. You are carried along by the current; otherwise you would stop at every pace, to gaze, to admire, and to covet.[23]

Some of the manufactures and warehouses required either a pre-booked visit or a small purchase to ensure admission and were included in guide-books to the metropolis.

Besides the professed collections of curiosities there are a variety of manufactures the property of private persons which are worthy of the notice of the public from their extent and novelty all of which may be viewed by permission easily obtained or by making a small purchase.[24]

The *Picture of London* listed several examples which covered a wide range of luxury goods including the Wedgwood warehouse in St James's Square (Figure 6.5), the Derby and Worcester China Warehouses in Covent Garden, Phillips and Christie's auction rooms and Mrs Lanchester's millinery and dress rooms in Sackville Street.

The luxurious well furnished and comfortable homes of middle and upper class residents did not go unnoticed, particularly by foreign visitors as Prince Pückler-Muskau remarked 'The technical part of social life – the arrangements for physical comfort and entertainment is well understood here.'[25] This even extended to modest middle-class housing and lodgings as a fellow German, von Raumer, observed when comparing London examples to those of his home country '... the hall and staircase of these houses [townhouses] are far more elegant ... . The stairs and floors are usually covered with handsome carpets, and even my lodging is not without its luxury.'[26]

The increasing number of merchants and other professionals who could now afford a house in town ensured a wide constituency for the vast range of modern consumable goods. On the opening of his London showroom

6.5   Wedgwood showroom, 1809

James Watt known equally for his manufacturing of steam engines and ormolu remarked that

We think it of far more consequence to supply the People than the nobility only … we think they will do more towards supporting a great Manufactory, than all the Lords in the nation.

The showrooms of London were then themselves sites of display with the added bonus that the cultural commodities on view were purchasable. Moreover, modern manufactures whether they drew on stylistic details from the past or embraced new technological advances became objects of desire. The display of knowledge, taste and, in the broadest sense, appreciation and 'ownership' of antiquity had been harnessed into the service of the propaganda machine of the social and cultural élite of Britain during the eighteenth century. The proliferation of shops, shopping arcades and other commercial outlets democratised the process of acquisition and appropriation of goods. These kinds of social activity were also open to women and this feminised the nature of urban experience and social life in London at this time. Indeed, the growth of the metropolis with all its new and complex sets of social relationships and the changing patterns of consumption and display ruptured the traditional social systems and reconfigured the relationship of society to the visual and material cultures of the past. In this way the city itself became a consumable object and this is nowhere more evident than in the medium of the print. Rudolph Ackermann's shop, The Repository of the Arts, at 101 Strand, was devoted to the production and sale of prints and colour plate books which celebrated the metropolis and urban life in the opening decades of the nineteenth century. Ackermann's best known endeavour is *The Microcosm of London* (1808–1810) a three-volume work which provided high quality colour views of the fashionable interiors and exteriors of London's best known buildings as well as topographical views of the city. It is a celebration of the metropolis which embraces the architecture, urban experience and social life of London and its residents whilst at the same time re-presenting the city as a spectacle for the viewing public. *The Microcosm* was available in 26 monthly instalments ensuring a wider audience for this highly ambitious project which helped develop the public's taste for the consumption of sights and sites of display.

Public consumption of the past

The rise of the public museum and the ordered display of artifacts from the past was a distinct development away from the generally less structured presentation of private collections in both town and country houses. But the practice of cultural self definition through reference to the past remained a fundamental element of these metropolitan displays. The Elgin Marbles remain one of the most contentious exhibits in the British Museum. In this context it is the question of the transference of the marbles from private to public ownership rather than the issue of cultural appropriation which helps map the viewing public's changing attitudes towards objects and their meaning. The marbles arrived in Britain piecemeal fashion between 1801 and 1811[27] and were first exhibited in Elgin's Museum – a mews connected to Lord Elgin's house on Park Lane for which a ticket of admission was required. From there the collection moved to a temporary structure at Burlington House. Although offered for sale to the nation in 1811 the marbles were only purchased in 1816 after a parliamentary enquiry followed by a vote in the House of Commons.[28] Alongside the recognition of their quality by Canova who visited London in 1815 the desirability of the marbles was enhanced by the Prince Regent's, later George IV, purchase for the nation of the Phygileian Marbles in 1814. These were displayed in a temporary addition to the British Museum which was then at Old Montague House, Bloomsbury, a late seventeenth-century 'private palace' (Figure 6.6). The artifacts formed the nucleus of the nation's collection of antiquities. But was a crumbling domestic structure with numerous additions an appropriate site to display these cultural riches?

The rise of national collections of antiquities, art and artifacts was a significant feature of the culture and society of the opening decades of the nineteenth century. For the first time government was prepared to commit substantial public funds for the purchase and display of large collections to enrich the nation's cultural and intellectual wealth. These national collections were agglomerations of private possessions – the Elgin Marbles provide just one example. A similar case in point is the acquisition by the National Gallery of the collections of John Julius Angerstein and Sir George Beaumont, both of which had been on display in their respective houses, in 1824 and 1827 respectively. The shift to public ownership bestowed on the nation the status and reputation that had previously been enjoyed by the private owner. And as these collections were now available to a wide-ranging public, restricted only by the admission policies of the institutions, there was a sense of empowerment at the accessibility of these objects. Both the British Museum and the National Gallery stood distinct from existing private institutions such as the Royal Academy or the Society of Dilettante in terms of their scope and funding, and by the fact that both national institutions were rehoused in the early nineteenth century in a specially designed building which formed an essential part of the new urban landscape. As part of the Metropolitan Improvements to London the new gallery and museum were adequately funded and helped shape the residents' and visitors' experience

6.6   James Stephanoff, An Apartment displaying the Phygileian Marbles and a
selection of the Elgin Marbles at Old Montague House, Bloomsbury, 1818. Coloured
aquatint

of the modern metropolis by their architecture and the status of their collections. The British Museum, despite its title, housed mainly objects from the
ancient world rather than Britain. It was not then a museum of the British
Isles but rather its collections reinforced the social and cultural hegemony of
the nation through the appropriated objects on display. Like the sights and
sites of commemoration which helped fashion the idea of the nation of
London this urban museum reinforced the notion of national superiority.
The new building (1823–1848) housed the ever-expanding national collection of antiquities as well as the King's Library which had belonged to
George III and was sold to the nation by his son George IV in 1821.[29] Its
imposing Greek Revival styling made reference at once to the bulk of the
museum's contents and contemporary trends in gallery design in Europe.
These elements combined to make the British Museum one of the sights of
Europe and this was a conscious achievement. Like the parliamentary reports

concerning the Metropolitan Improvements those relating to the design and methods of display of the British Museum make continual references to the development of the Louvre in Paris and how this might be surpassed.[30] In concert with the Louvre and other European examples the British Museum adopted a linear method of displaying its collection where the visitor was obliged to follow a prescribed route through the whole collection. The didactic nature of the displays of the objects in the British Museum was a microcosm of the viewing process of the city itself. The defined route through the museum and the consequent way in which the collection was encountered echoed the rationalisation of the street plan and the development of sites and sights of commemoration which had re-shaped urban experience. The National Gallery, which despite its title held few pictures by indigenous artists, was a fitting pendant piece to the British Museum.[31] Situated on the north side of what became Trafalgar Square on the former site of the Royal Mews, the gallery formed an essential part of the refashioning of Charing Cross. Moreover, its central location reaffirmed the importance of culture – or perhaps its conspicuous consumption and display – to the new metropolitan society. The public ownership and the relatively easy accessibility of these national collections were important. But this sense of empowerment at the mapping of the past was an essential part of the broader power systems which operated in the early nineteenth-century metropolis. The rationalisation of the streetplan and the panoptic regime of the flâneur/euse were systems of viewing that engendered feelings of order and control. These were translated into the public museum and so served to reinforce the social and cultural systems of the metropolitan viewing public. Moreover, this kind of consumption was ungendered as the museum was frequented by both male and female spectators. Knowledge was indeed power for the middle classes and the ordering of the past into coherent displays was part of the rationalising process of democratising power structures.

Knowledge is power

The practice of ordering knowledge and the presentation of displays of cultural values extended beyond the confines of national institutions to have a more general impact on the nature of urban experience in early nineteenth-century London. The Regent's Park came increasingly to represent the modern metropolis in terms of its planning, demography and the social interchange it encouraged. The park was one of the most popular places to promenade or to ride, to see and be seen and to admire, covet or display fashion, taste and wealth. It was in many ways the natural habitat of the flâneur/euse with its fine villas and landscaped parkland. But there were other distractions to

6.7   Decimus Burton, View of Regent's Park Zoo (with the Regent's Park Terraces in the background), 1829

both amuse the urban bourgeoisie and provide a platform for the social rituals and cultural practices that defined their caste. Two distinct land-scaped spaces: the Zoological Society Gardens (1826–41) and the Royal Botanical Society Gardens (1840–59) made a substantial contribution to the social environment of the park for residents and visitors (Figure 6.7). The purpose here is not to re-tell their development and building procedure – this has been done elsewhere[32] – but rather to underline the varied and didactic nature of urban experience and social life in the early nineteenth-century metropolis.

The Royal Zoological Society was founded by Sir Stanford Raffles in July 1824. It comprised 151 members including residents of the Regent's Park – of whom the Marquis of Hertford was amongst their number. Although the Society had premises in Bruton Street an open air menagerie was required for the growing collection of living specimens and the king's private zoo which had been housed in inadequate accommodation at the Tower of London. The park was the obvious spot but the preferred site of the inner circle had been let to the nurseryman Mr Jenkins. Instead Decimus Burton was engaged to landscape an irregular, triangular shaped site of five acres in the north-east corner of the park which was bisected by the Outer Circle. Burton's clever use of a tunnel to link the two features is still in use today. And his

PULAR GARDENS.-TOM, JERRY *and* LOGIC *laughing at the bustle and alarm occasioned amongst the Visitor the escape of a Kangaroo, the 'Fat Knight' down on the subject*

6.8 R. Cruikshank, Popular Gardens – Tom, Jerry *and* Logic *laughing at the bustle and alarm occasioned amongst the Visitors by the escape of a Kangaroo, the 'Fat Knight' down on the subject,* 1821

innovative designs for animal houses including a clock tower which was part of the camel house and the giraffe house add to the quality of the spectacle.[33] The display of living natural history was a popular and impressive attraction even to those who were at liberty to enjoy the full range of metropolitan spectacles (Figure 6.8):

> I rode in … Regent's Park … and visited the menagerie lately established there, which presents a model worthy of imitation. There is nothing overdone, and at the same time a neatness, which assuredly can be attained nowhere but in England. Here I saw a tiger-cat, a creature which seemed to me a perfect model of beauty and elegance among quadrupeds.[34]

The Royal Botanical Society was founded in 1838 with J. D. C. Sowerbey as Secretary. It took over the grounds in the inner circle of the park, originally let to Mr Jenkins.[35] Burton was again appointed architect in 1840 and with the help of Mr Marnock, the curator of the plant collection, laid out the grounds on a Linnaean arrangement, including medical, agricultural and manufacturing gardens, at the considerable cost of £12,000. Burton's final design included high turfed mounds along the paths with appropriate breaks to allow views through the whole layout. The high banks were to be made possible in part by the materials removed in the excavation of a lake. Both these elements were 'to render the Inner Circle more pleasing to the Public who are likely in consequence of the alterations in the Park to be more frequent visitors to the Inner Circle'. The gardens did prove a popular attraction and unlike the Zoological Gardens they were freely open to the general public.

There is no doubt that the Regent's Park and the metropolis as a whole were exposed to an ever-expanding public during the opening decades of the nineteenth century. The increase in home tourism coupled with a growing interest in architecture meant that the urban environment was of interest to many levels of society and became a benchmark of class difference, social aspirations and architectural criticism. As such the metropolis represented notions of national identity which were understood and interpreted by its foreign and British publics. The guidebooks to London ranged from ephemeral, simply printed 'guides' to elaborate illustrated publications celebrating the sights of the city, and even catalogues of collections in great detail. The importance of public and private collections was a common theme. But beyond this the visitor or viewer was encouraged to take in the sites of London – whether they be architecture or landscape – as part of the experience of the metropolis. And it is on this theme that the Regent's Park offered its most appropriate attraction – Thomas Hornor's Colosseum (1823–7). For a small fee the visitor entered a constructed illusion of his/her own urban environment. As the hydraulic lift ascended, the false perspective of the city, of which the viewer was a constituent part, came into focus re-presenting the metropolis, its architecture, urban experience and social life.

Notes

1. The relationship between objects and social values is discussed by Pierre Bourdieu, *The Field of Cultural Production*, Oxford, Polity Press, 1993.

2. On this point see my chapter 'The Illusion of Grandeur? antiquity, Grand Tourism and the country house' in D. Arnold, *The Georgian Country House: architecture, landscape and society*, Stroud and New York, Sutton Publishing, 1998, 100–16.

3. The Grove is fully discussed in my chapter 'A Family Affair: Decimus Burton's designs for the Regent's Park villas' in D. Arnold (ed.) *The Georgian Villa*, Stroud and New York, Sutton Publishing, 1998, 105–17.

4. This was executed by J. Henning, a member of Decimus Burton's regular workforce. Henning had made casts of the Elgin Marbles when they were housed in the courtyard of the Royal Academy on their arrival in London.

5. St Dunstan's is fully discussed in my chapter 'A Family Affair: Decimus Burton's designs for the Regent's Park villas' in D. Arnold (ed.), *loc. cit.*

6. A folio volume containing the ten drawings Burton exhibited at the Royal Academy is in the collection of the Architectural Association.

7. E. M. Butler (ed.) *A Regency Visitor, The English Tour of Prince Pückler-Muskau Described in his letters 1826–1828*, London, Collins, 1957, letter dated 7 April 1827, 187.

8. At the beginning of the period this also related to the value of each property. In 1798 Chatsworth was estimated to be worth £22,322 whereas Devonshire House was valued at £29,286.

9. On this point see M. H. Port 'Town house and Country House: their interaction' in D. Arnold (ed.), *The Georgian Country House: architecture, landscape and society, op. cit.*

10. Townley's Collection is discussed in C. Fox (ed.) *London World City 1800–1840*, New Haven and London, Yale University Press, 1992, 432–6.

11. For a full discussion of Hope's Duchess Street mansion see D. Watkin, *Thomas Hope and the Neo-classical Idea*, London, Murray, 1968. The house was purchased by Hope in 1799 and remodelled in 1800. A picture gallery was added in 1819.

12. E. M. Butler *op. cit.*, letter dated 5 December 1826, 94.

13. Soane was Professor of Architecture at the Royal Academy and his collection complemented his lectures see D. Watkin, *Sir John Soane and Enlightenment Thought, The Royal Academy Lectures* Cambridge, Cambridge University Press, 1996.

14. A. Penrose, *The Autobiography and Memoirs of Benjamin Robert Haydon (1786–1846)* compiled from his 'autobiography and journals' and 'correspondence and table-talk', G. Bell & Sons, London, 1927, Ch XXIII Letter to Miss Mitford, 28 March 1825, 305–7.

15. The houses are discussed in Sir John Summerson, *The Life and Work of John Nash, Architect*, London and Cambridge, Mass., 1980, 132–3 and T. Davis, *John Nash, the Prince Regent's Architect*, London, South Brunswick and New York, A. S. Barnes, 1967, 77–9.

16. This was illustrated in A. Pugin and J. Britton, *Public Buildings of London*, 1827. It was a popular attraction in the metropolis although Nash only granted admittance to upper class visitors including Prince Puckler-Muskau. See Davis, *op. cit.*, 77–9. Davis also mentions a separate Gallery of Architecture in the house but no further details about this have come to light.

17. E. M. Butler (ed.), *op. cit.*, letter dated 14 July 1827, 231.

18. *Survey of London*, XX, Trafalgar Square and the Parish of St Martin in the Fields, III, 68.

19. These were donated by Decimus Burton to the Victoria and Albert Museum in 1879. The casts are now held in storage in the sculpture archive and numbered V&A 1879–19 to 1879–266.

20. Held in a private collection.

21. See *Survey of London*, XX, III, 68.

22. William Darton, *A Description of London*, London, 1824, 7.

23. *Letters from Albion to a friend on the Continent, written in the years 1810, 1811, 1812, and 1813*, London, 1814.

24. *The Picture of London*, London, 1802, 371.

25. E. M. Butler *op. cit.*, letter dated 25 March 1827, 180.

26. Frederick von Raumer, *England in 1835*, trans. by S. Austin, 2 vols, London, 1836, 1, 12 April 1835, 99.

27. The Elgin Marbles are discussed in F. H. Taylor, *The Taste of Angels, A History of Collecting from Rameses to Napoleon*, London, Hamish Hamilton, 1948, 497–510 and A. R. Smith, 'Lord Elgin and his Collection', *Journal of Hellenic Studies*, II, 1916.

28. The quality and authenticity of the marbles were the subjects of heated debate between Richard Payne Knight and B. R. Haydon. See A. Penrose, *The Autobiography and Memoirs of Benjamin Robert Haydon (1786–1846)* compiled from his 'autobiography and journals' and 'correspondence and table-talk', London, G. Bell & Sons, 1927.

29. The British Museum also housed for a short time the nation's pictures and natural history collection. For a full discussion of the rebuilding of the museum see J. Mordaunt Crook, The British Museum, London, Allen Lane, 1972.

30. Parliamentary Report into the British Museum.

31. For a full discussion of William Wilkins' design for the National Gallery see R. Liscombe, *William Wilkins 1778–1839*, Cambridge, Cambridge University Press, 1980.

32. See P. Chalmers Mitchell, *The Zoological Society of London Centenary History*, London, The Zoological Society, 1929.

33. Burton's design success was such that he was asked to design the Zoological Society Gardens in the Phoenix Park, Dublin.

34. E. M. Butler *op. cit.*, letter dated 27 March 1828, 308–9.

35. See G. Meynell, 'The Royal Botanic Society's Gardens, Regent's Park', *The London Journal*, 6 (2), 1980.

Postscript

London is fundamental to our understanding of the complex social, cultural and economic interrelationships of the period 1800–1840 in Britain. This volume has attempted to subvert the notion of a single viewpoint of these relationships, whether it be methodological, historical or authorial, which colours the way in which the metropolis is seen. Underpinning this book is an assertion of Wittgenstein's: that it is impossible to say anything about the world as a whole as we are only able to do this if we are able to get outside it – which we clearly cannot do as we cannot conceive of anything beyond our world. If this idea is applied to the discussion of a cultural icon like the modern metropolis of London 1800–1840 it presents the proposition that we are unable to detach ourselves from it as it is part of our world. Because it is within the realm of the architectural historian's experience the historian cannot see it as a whole. Moreover, as the evidence in the chapters suggest, this was also the case for the contemporary resident and visitor to the metropolis. And it is their fractured experience of the city which remains a fundamental touchstone of this study. This presents the notion that our knowledge and understanding will always be fragmentary and subjective, providing only glimpses of the entire picture. And this is what each of the chapters or 'walks' around London has attempted to do – the metropolis is re-presented in a range of thematic explorations which reveals at once the resonances and dissonances of its various images and identities.

Given this framework for understanding is it possible to define my role as an architectural historian or indeed my role as a narrator or interlocutor between the metropolis and the reader? The answer may lie in Wittgenstein's view of himself as taking his readers on a tour bus along the intellectual routes which make up the map of the problem of language and under-standing.[1] In this way I have acted as a kind of 'tour guide'. Is it then my role to guide us through the different paths of interpretation of the early nineteenth-century metropolis and to supply signposts which you, the reader, are to follow? This would imply a flawless relationship between what we think, how we say it and the way in which it is understood. This is the central theme of Wittgenstein's concerns as he conjectures that a single thought is expressed by a single word and explores the relationship between thought and word in terms of which predicates the other. Moreover, if I, as the historian, am supplying signposts can it be assumed that there is only one way for you, the reader, to read them? Should you follow the finger of the signpost or go in the opposite direction? Both directions lead somewhere. Each of the chapters has provided a series of signposts providing a route through a particular theme relevant to the architecture, urban experience and social life of London 1800–1840. But the intention has been to show how it is possible to follow other routes as each chapter runs parallel to and intersects with the others. In doing this I have resisted the temptation to represent the city as a model of chronological progression and change as this kind of historical determinism only works if there are no alternatives and the avoidance of deterministic narratives is a fundamental part of the method of this book. Instead the emphasis has been placed on temporal discontinuities and subjective responses to the metropolis 1800–1840 as expressed by its contemporaries. London has then been re-presented as a constantly changing and developing entity evading the static definitions of deterministic histories. In this way the historian can respond to the changing functions of the city and the space it both occupies and creates whilst at the same time being aware that the city itself is a self consciously constructed artefact. In identifying and exploring the complexities of the metropolis the unknowable totality of the whole has in some ways been brought down to a human scale. But one fundamental question remains unresolved: what is London? Is it perhaps the geographical site, the experiential sight or the social spectacle? In other words what is the original and what is being re-presented? How does the panorama of the Colosseum relate to the metropolis it represents? (See Figure 1.2 on page 3). Perhaps Jacques Derrida can offer some clarification:

That which is, being-present (the matrix-form of substance, of reality, of the opposition between matter and form, essence and existence, objectivity and subjectivity, etc.) is distinguished from the appearance, the image, the phenomenon. etc., that is from anything that, presenting it as being present, doubles it, re-presents it, and can therefore replace and de-present it. ... The image supervenes upon reality, the representation upon the present in presentation, the imitation upon the thing, the imitator upon the imitated. First there is what is 'reality', the thing itself, in flesh and blood as the phenomenologists say; then there is, imitating these, the painting, the portrait, the zographeme, the inscription or transcription of the thing itself. Discernability, at least numerical discernability, between imitator and the imitated is what constitutes order. And obviously, according to 'logic' itself, according to a profound synonymy, what is imitated is more real, more essential, more true, etc., than what imitates.[2]

But somehow I think my question requires more than one answer. ...

Notes

1. For a fuller discussion see D. Arnold 'Wittgenstein and the Country House', *Society of Architectural Historians of Great Britain Newsletter*, No 58 Summer 1996, pp. 1–2. Wittgenstein's ideas are set out in his *Tractatus Logico-Philosophicus* and his later work *Philosophical Investigations*.

2. Jacques Derrida, *Dissemination*, Chicago, University of Chicago Press, 1981 p. 191.

Appendix
An Inventory of Casts owned by Decimus Burton taken from a handwritten inventory delivered with the casts on their being donated by Burton to the Victoria and Albert Museum in 1879

An inventory of casts collected by Mr Brown in Italy, delivered at Mr Dec Burton's office 14 Spring Gardens November 1827

TEMPLE OF MARS ULTOR

1   Helice of the Capital with returning angle
2   Flower in centre of Abacus
3   Lower leaf of Capital
4   Flower in centre of Coffer
5   Two parts of second leaf Capital

PANTHEON

6   Capital in the Portico
7   Part of Cornice
8   Modillion Coffer and Flower in do
9   Ornamental panel with Candelabrum
10   do do do
11   Attic capital

12
13   Roman Eagle and Wreath from a Marble in the atrium of the Church of St Apostoli
14

15   Part of the Tomb of Scipio
16   do
17   do

18   do

TEMPLE OF JUPITER TONANS

19   Soffit Panel
20   Part of Cornice
21   Modillion
22   Part of Architrave
23   Flower in centre of Coffer
24

TEMPLE OF VESTA AT TIVOLI

25   Part of the frieze
26
27   Part of the capital
28

TRAJAN'S FORUM

29   large Ovolo Moulding
30   do Ogee do enriched
31   do
32

CHURCH OF ST GREGORY

33   Small Corinthian capital
34 } Part of a base enriched
35

VILLA MEDICI

36   Festoons of Fruit Flowers & Ox's Head
37   do
38   do
39   A Pilaster from the Garden
40   do
41   do
42

TEMPLE OF JUPITER STATOR

43   Modillion
44   Lower Leaf of Capital
45   Stem and Part of Helice of do
46   Part of Abacus of do
47   Part of cornice with Lion's head
48   Another part of do
49   The Coffer Panel with Flower
50   Part of Architrave Moulding
51   Another part of do
52   Another part of do
53

TRAJAN'S COLUMN

54   Base Moulding of Pedestal
55   Cap do
56   Part of festoon of do
57   Part of the Torus of column
58

TEMPLE OF ANTONINUS AND FAUSTINA

59   part of frieze
60   do
61   do
62   do
63   do
64   do
65   Part of the Cornice
66   Lower Part of the capital
67   Another do
68

TEMPLE OF VESTA AT ROME

69   A fragment now in the Vatican
70   do
71

VILLA ADRIAN

72 part of Column Capital
73 A Pilaster [capital]
74 A Fragment
75

VILLA PONIATONSKI [BURTON'S SPELLING]

76 Part of a frieze
77 do
78 do and Architrave
79 A Golochi
80 part of an ornamental panel
81 do

VILLA ALBANI

83 Bust of a Cariatide
84 A Mask
85 A do
86 A Fragment
87
88 Part of a large Vase from the Campadoria
89 The Hand of Flora from do

THE VATICAN

90
91
92
93 Part of a Candelabrum
94 do
95 do
97 do
98 do
99 do
100 do
101 A Candelabrum in basso Relievo of the Cinque Centoage [sixteenth century]
102 A Chimera and Ornament
103 A do

104	A do
105	A do
106	A do
107	A do
108	A do Leg and Ornamental
109	A do Head (very spirited)
110	Part Of A Base With Plinth Enriched
111	do enriched
112	A Pilaster capital
114	A do
115	A do
116	A do
117	Part of the Cornice of a Tomb
118	Part of a Vase
119	do
120	do
121	do
122	do
123	Part of a Vase
124	A Pilaster and capital
125	A do of the Cinque Cento age
126	do
127	Part of a frieze (Griffin and Foliage)
128	do
129	do
130	An Antefix
131	A Chimera Leg
132	A Standard with terminal Figures and ornament
133	A Modillion
134	A do
135	Part of a Truss
136	do
137	A panel ornamented with Cornucopia
138	Part of a Pilaster
139	do
140	do
141	do
142	do
143	Front of a sarcophagus (Griffin and Foliage)
144	A Basso Relievo (the Provinces)
145	Part of a Frieze (Griffin Candelabrum and foliage)
146	A Small Corinthian Column

147	a do
148	An Angle of a Square Tazza
149	Front of a Cippus
150	Part of a Panel
151	Top end of a Pilaster
152	A Panel (Boy and Foliage)
153	A do
154	Half the body of a car
155	A Sphinx
156	A griffin in Basso Relievo
157	A Statue of Ceres
158	One face of the Tripod of a Candelabrum
159	do
160	A Fragment
161	A do
162	A do
163	A do
164	A do
165	A do
166	A do
167	A do
168	A do
169	A do
170	A Frieze, ornamented with Cornucopia and Foliage (very rich)
171	A frieze (Boy and Festoons of Fruit) from a Terra Cotta
172	A do
173	A do
174	A do
175	A do
176	A Fragment [Villa Pamphili added in a different hand look like an aged Burton's]
177	A do
178	A do
179	A do
180	A do
181	A do
182	A do
183	A do [Villa Poniatowski added in a different hand look like an aged Burton's]
184	A Basso Relievo (Greek)
185	A do
186	A do

187   A Lion's Head
188   Part of the Cornice of the Arch of Septimus Severus
189
190   A Patera from Pazzolo
191   A do
192   A do
194   A do
195   Front of an Ionic Capital (very rich) from the Church of St Mary in Trastvere
196   Flank of do
197   do
198   A Fragment from the Church of St Pietro in Vincoli
199   A Piece of Ornament from the Villa Pamp[h]ili
200   A do
201   A do Church of the Peace
202   A do
203   A Basso Relievo (Romulus and Remus)
204
205   Part of an Ionic Capital from the Temple of Erectheus
206   The Antai from do
207   Part of a Corinthian capital from the Temple of the Winds
208   Part of a Cippus
209   do

List of casts ordered from Rome, Novr 1838

1   One Quarter of a Candelabrum in the Museum of the Vatican
2   One Quarter of another Candelabrum from the Vatican
3   One Candelabrum entire
4   Portion of Frieze from the Forum of Trajan
5   do
6   do
7   A Boy and Vase (from the Vatican)
8   One half of an Antefix from the Collection of the Villa Pamphili
9   A Coffer and Rosette
10   Enriched Ovolo Moulding
11   Ornamental Pilaster
12
13
14} Six Figures forming sides of the Tripod Candelabrum

15
17
       A Table, on moveable stand 5 × 3½

Bibliography

Manuscript sources

The principal sources were:

Records of the Crown Estate Office held at the Public Record Office in London indicated by the prefix Cres.

Records of the Office of Public Works held at the Public Record Office in London indicated by the prefix Work.

Drawings relating to the Records of the Offices of Woods and Works held at the Public Record Office in London indicated by the prefixes MPE and MPI.

Treasury Minutes held at the Public Record Office in London indicated by the prefix T29.

Other sources in London are held at:

The Bedford Estate Office
The British Museum
The Royal Institute of British Architects Drawings Collection and Library
Sir John Soane's Museum
The Victoria and Albert Museum
Westminster Library
The private collection of James and Decimus Burton's descendants

Parliamentary papers

The Surveyor General's Triennial Report, 1809
Report of the Commissioners of His Majesty's Woods, Forests and Land Revenues, 1812

Report of the Commissioners of His Majesty's Woods, Forests and Land Revenues, 1826

Report from the Select Committee on the Office of Works, 1828

Report from the Select Committee on Windsor Castle and Buckingham Palace, 1831

Report from the Select Committee on Public Walks, 1833

Report of the Commissioners of Her Majesty's Woods, Forests and Land Revenues, 1835

Report from the Select Committee appointed to enquire into the plan sanctioned by the Commissioners of Woods and Forests for laying out the vacant space in Trafalgar Square, in front of the National Gallery, 1840

Contemporary sources

CONTEMPORARY JOURNALS AND COMMENTARIES ON LONDON
Specific references to volumes of contemporary journals are cited in the main text.

Autobiography
The Builder Civil Engineer and Architects' Journal
Gardener's Magazine
Gentleman's Magazine
Mechanics' Magazine
New Monthly Magazine
The Plain Speaker
Tegg's Magazine

CONTEMPORARY GUIDEBOOKS AND COMMENTARIES ON LONDON

The Ambulator, London, 1811

Barjaud, J. B. B. and Landon, C. P., *Description de Londres et de ses environs*, Paris, 1810

Britton, J., *A Brief Account of the Colosseum*, London, 1829

—— and Pugin, A., *The Public Buildings of London*, London, 1825.

Crutwell, Richard, *Remarks on the Buildings and Improvements in London and Elsewhere*, London, 1816

Darton, William, *A Description of London: a sketch of the history and present state and almost all celebrated public buildings*, London, 1824

Dobie, R., *A History of the United Parishes of St Giles in the Fields and St George's Bloomsbury*, London, 1829

Egan, Pierce, *Life in London: the Day and Night Scenes of Jerry Hawthorn Esq. and his elegant friend Corinthian Tom, accompanied by Bob Logic, the Oxonian, in their Rambles and Sprees through the Metropolis*, London, 1821

Elmes, J., *Metropolitan Improvements: or London in the nineteenth century*, London, 1827–8

Evelyn, John, *Fumifugium*, London, 1661

Heinrich, Heine, *English Fragments*, 1828

Hornor, T., *Four engravings*, London, 1822

Hunter, Revd Henry, *History of London and its environs*, 2 vols, London, 1811

Lambert, B., *The History and Survey of London*, 4 vols, London, 1806

Leigh's *New Picture of London*, London, 1820

London Lions for Country Cousins and Friends about Town, New Buildings, improvements and amusements in the British Metropolis Illustrated with wood engravings by Horace Wellbeloved, London, 1826

Malcolm, J., *Londinium Redivivum*, London, 1802–1807

Mudie, Robert, *Babylon the Great*, London, 1825

The Picture of London, 3rd edn, London, 1815

White, J., *Some account of the proposed improvements of the western part of London, by the formation of the Regent's Park, the New Street, the new sewer, &c, &c: illustrated by a variety of plans and accompanied by explanatory and critical observations*, London, 1815

Books and articles

Abbey, J., *Scenery of Great Britain and Ireland*, 1770–1860, London, Dawsons, 1972

Ackermann, R., *The Microcosm of London*, 1804

Adams, B., *London Illustrated, 1604–1851*, London, Library Association, 1983

Adorno, T., 'Veblen's Attack on Culture', *Prisms*, London, Spearman, 1967

Allen, R., *The Moving Pageant: a literary source book on London street-life, 1700–1914*, London and New York, Routledge, 1998

Altick, R., *The Shows of London*, Cambridge, Mass., Harvard University Press, 1978

Andrews, M., *The Search for the Picturesque: landscape, aesthetics and tourism in Britain 1760–1800*, Aldershot, Ashgate, 1989

—— 'A Picturesque Template: the tourists and their guidebooks' in D. Arnold (ed.) *The Picturesque in late Georgian England*, London, The Georgian Group, 1995, 3–9

Arnold, D., 'The Arch at Constitution Hill: a new axis for London', *Apollo*, CXXXVIII (379), September 1993, 129–33

—— 'Decimus Burton and the Urban Picturesque', in D. Arnold (ed.) *The Picturesque in late Georgian England*, London, The Georgian Group, 1995, 51–6

—— *The Georgian Country House: architecture, landscape and society*, Stroud and New York, Sutton Publishing, 1998

—— (ed.) *The Georgian Villa*, Stroud and New York, Sutton Publishing, 1998

—— (ed.) *The Metropolis and its Image: constructing identities for London c 1750–1950* The Association of Art Historians and Blackwell, Oxford, 1999

—— 'Paris Haussman: Le Pari d'Haussman', *Architects' Journal*, 13 November 1991

—— 'Rationality, Safety and Power: the street planning of later Georgian London', *Georgian Group Journal*, London, 1995

Aspinall, A., *The Correspondence of George IV*, Cambridge, Cambridge University Press, 1952

Ballantyne, A., (ed.) *Architecture and Sacrifice*, forthcoming

Bamford, F. and the Duke of Wellington (eds) *The Journal of Mrs Arbuthnot 1820–1832*, London, Macmillan, 1950

Barker, F. and Hyde, R., *London as it Might Have Been*, London, John Murray, 1982

—— and Jackson, P., *London: 200 years of a city and its people*, London, Cassell, 1974

Bataille, G., *The Accursed Share: an essay on general economy*, trans. R. Hurley, New York, Zone, 1991

de Beer, E. S., (ed.) *John Evelyn: London revived*, Oxford, Clarendon Press, 1938

Bell, A., *London in the Age of Dickens*, Norman, University of Oklahoma Press, 1967

Benjamin, W., 'Paris – Capital of the Nineteenth Century', *Reflections*, trans. E. Jephcott, New York, Harcourt, Brace and Jovanovich, 1979
—— 'Central Park', *New German Critique*, 34, Winter 1985
Bingham, N., (ed.) *The Education of the Architect, Proceedings of the 22nd Annual Symposium of the Society of Architectural Historians of Great Britain*, London, Society of Architectural Historians of Great Britain, 1993
Bullen, R., *The Foreign Office, 1782–1982*, Frederick, MD., University Publishers of London, Maryland, 1984
Burke, E., *An Analytical Enquiry into the Origin of our Ideas of the Sublime and the Beautiful*, London, 1757
Butler E. M., (ed) *A Regency Visitor, The English Tour of Prince Pückler-Muskau Described in his letters 1826–1828*, London, Collins, 1957
Cannadine, D., 'The Context. Performance and Meaning of Ritual: the British monarchy and the 'invention of tradition', c 1820–1977' in E. Hobsbawn and T. Ranger (eds) *The Invention of Tradition*, Cambridge, Cambridge University Press, 1983
de Certeau, M., *The Practice of Everyday life*, Berkeley, University of California Press, 1984
Colley, L., *Britons, the Forging of a Nation*, New Haven and London, Yale University Press, 1992
Colvin, H., *A Biographical Dictionary of Architects*, 3rd edn, New Haven and London, Yale University Press, 1995
Cook, D., 'The Townley Marbles in Westminster and Bloomsbury', The British Museum Yearbook, 2, 1977, BM Publications, London
Copley, S. and Garside, P. (eds) *The Politics of the Picturesque*, Cambridge and New York, Cambridge University Press, 1994
Crook, J. Mordaunt, 'The Villas in Regent's Park (1) & (2)', *Country Life*, 143, 1968
—— and Port, M. H., *The History of the King's Works*, VI, London, HMSO, 1970
Daniels, S., *Fields of Vision*, Oxford, Polity Press, 1986
Davis, T., *The Architecture of John Nash*, London, Studio, 1960
Defoe, Daniel, *The Fortunes and Misfortunes of the Famous Moll Flanders*, London, 1722
Deutsch, Karl, *Nation and Society*, Cambridge, Mass., MIT, 1966
Dyos, H. J. and Wolff, M. (eds) *The Victorian City: images and realities*, London, Routledge and Kegan Paul, 1976
Farington, J., *Diary 1793–1821*, ed. K. Garlick and A. MacIntyre, London and New Haven, Yale University Press, 1978
Feldman, D., *Metropolis: London, histories and representations since 1800*, London, Routledge, 1989
Foucault, M., *Discipline and Punish: the birth of the prison*, trans from (*Surveiller et Punir*), London, Penguin, 1979
Foucault, M., *Politics, Philosophy, Culture*, ed. L. D. Kritzman, New York, Routledge, 1988
—— *The Order of Things: an archaeology of human sciences*, London, Tavistock, 1970
—— *The Archaeology of Knowledge*, London, Routledge, 1990
—— *Of Other Spaces*, Diacritics, Spring, 1986
Fox, C. (ed.) *London – World City 1800–1840*, New Haven and London, Yale University Press, 1992
Freer, A., *John Nash: The Delighted Eye*, Aldershot, Scolar Press, 1993
Freud, S., 'Civilization and its Discontents' in *Civilization, Society and Religion*, Dickson, A. ed., Penguin Freud Library, 12, Harmondsworth, Penguin, 1991

Gash, Norman (ed) *Wellington: studies in the military and political career of the first Duke of Wellington*, Manchester, Manchester University Press in association with the University of Southampton, 1990

Geidion, S., *Space, Time and Architecture*, Cambridge, Mass., Harvard University Press, 1971

Gilpin, W., *Three Essays:- on Picturesque Beauty;- on Picturesque travel; and, on Sketching Landscape: to which is added a Poem on Landscape Painting*, London, 1792

Girouard, M., *Cities and People*, New Haven and London, Yale University Press, 1985

Graves, A., *The Royal Academy – A complete dictionary of contributors 1769–1904*, London, H. Graves & Co., 1970

Hazlitt, William, 'On Londoners and Country People', *New Monthly Magazine*, August 1823

—— 'On Londoners and Country People', *The Plain Speaker*, 1826

Hemingway, A., *Landscape Imagery and Urban Culture in Early C19th Britain*, Cambridge, Cambridge University Press, 1992

Hibbert, C., *George IV*, Harmondsworth, Penguin, 1976

Hipple, W., *The Beautiful, the Sublime and the Picturesque in Eighteenth-century British Aesthetic Theory*, Illinois, Southern Illinois University Press, 1957

Hobhouse, H., *A History of Regent Street*, London, MacDonald and Janes, Queen Anne Press, 1975

Hobsbawn, E. (ed.) 'Inventing Tradition', *The Invention of Tradition*, Cambridge, Cambridge University Press, 1983

Holliday, J., *An Appeal to the Governors of the Foundling Hospital and the probable consequences of covering hospital lands with buildings*, London, 1787

—— *A Further Appeal to the Governors of the Foundling Hospital and justification of their conduct in not having covered the hospital lands with buildings since the institution of the charity*, London, 1788

Honour, Hugh, 'The Regent's Park Colosseum', *Country Life*, 2 January 1953

Hyde, R., *Gilded Scenes and Shining Prospects – Panoramic Views of British Towns 1575–1900*, Yale Center for British Art, New Haven, Connecticut, 1985

Jeffery, S., *The Mansion House*, Chichester, The Corporation of London and Phillimore and Co., 1993

Jones, R. L., *Reminiscences of the Public Life of Richard Lambert Jones Esq.*, London, 1863

Jones, R. P., 'The Life and Work of Decimus Burton', *Architectural Review*, 1905

Kostof, S., *The City Shaped*, London, Thames and Hudson, 1991

Lambert, B., *The History and Survey of London*, 4 vols, London, 1806

Langford, P., *A Polite and Commercial People*, Oxford, Oxford University Press, 1989

Lefebvre, H., *The Production of Space*, Oxford, Basil Blackwell, 1991

Liscombe, R. W., *William Wilkins 1778–1839*, Cambridge, Cambridge University Press, 1980

Loudon, J. C., *Encyclopaedia of Gardening*, London, 1822

—— *The Landscape Gardening and Landscape Architecture of the late Humphry Repton Esq. being his entire works on these subjects*, London, 1840

McCalman, Iain, 'Ultra Radicalism and Convivial Debating Clubs in London, 1795–1838', *English Historical Review*, 1987

McCullen, J. and Arnold, B., *Decimus Burton Exhibition*, Dublin, Institute of Landscape Horticulture of Ireland, 1988

Mace, R., *Trafalgar Square: emblem of Empire*, London, Lawrence and Wishart, 1976

Malcolm, E. H., 'London Coffee Houses and their Customers', *Tegg's Magazine*, 1, 1844

Malcolm, J., *Londinium Redivivum*, London, 1802–7

Malden, J., *John Henning 1771–1851*, Paisley, Renfrew District Council Museum and Art Galleries, 1977

Mansbridge, M., *John Nash: the complete catalogue*, Oxford, Phaidon, 1991

Massey, Doreen, 'Flexible Sexism', *Society and Space*, 9(1), 1991

Meynell, G., 'The Royal Botanic Society's Gardens, Regent's Park', *London Journal*, 6(2), 1980.

Miller, P., *Decimus Burton 1800–1881 Exhibition Catalogue*, London, The Building Centre Trust, 1981

Mitchell, P. Chalmers, *The Zoological Society of London Centenary History*, London, The Zoological Society, 1929

Morris R. J., (ed.) *The Victorian City: a reader in British urban history, 1820–1914*, London, Longman, 1993

Mumford, L., *The City in History*, Harmondsworth, Penguin, 1991

—— *City Development*, London, Secker and Warburg, 1973

Olsen, D. J., *The City as a Work of Art, London, Paris, Vienna*, New Haven and London, Yale University Press, 1986

—— *The Growth of Victorian London*, London, Batsford, 1976

—— *Town Planning in London*, 2nd edn, New Haven and London, Yale University Press, 1982

Penrose, A., *The Autobiography and Memoirs of Benjamin Robert Haydon (1786–1846) compiled from his 'autobiography and journals' and 'correspondence and table-talk'*, London, G. Bell & Sons, 1927

Percy, S. and Percy, R., *The Percy History and Interesting memorial on the rise, progress and present state of all the capitals of Europe*, 3 vols, London, 1823

Physick, J., *The Wellington Monument*, London, HMSO, 1970

Picon, A., *French Architects and Engineers in the Age of Enlightenment*, Cambridge, Cambridge University Press, 1992

Place, Francis, 'The Street Charing Cross', *Autobiography*, 1835

Pool, B. (ed.), *The Croker Papers: 1808–1857*, London, 1967

Port, M. H., 'George IV's Houses' in D. Arnold (ed.) *Squanderous and Lavish Profusion: George IV, his image and patronage of the arts*, London, The Georgian Group, 1995

—— *The Palace of Westminster*, New Haven and London, Yale University Press, 1976

Price, U., *Essay on the Picturesque*, London, 1792

—— *Essays on the Picturesque*, London, 1794

Pugin, A. W. N., *The Microcosm of London*, London, Penguin, 1943

Rasmussen, S. E., *London the Unique City*, 2nd edn, Cambridge, Mass., MIT Press, 1982

Ribeiro, A., *Dress and Morality*, London, Holmes and Meier, 1986

Rothenstein, J., *John Nash*, London, MacDonald, 1983

Royal Institute of British Architects, *Catalogue of the Drawings Collection*, Farnborough, RIBA, 1969–76

Ruffinière du Prey, P., *Sir John Soane: the making of an architect*, Chicago, University of Chicago Press, 1982

Sadler, T. (ed.) *Henry Crabb Robinson, Diary, 1872*, London, Macmillan, 1869

Samuel, E. C., *The Villas in Regent's Park and their Residents*, London, Bedford College, 1959

Saunders, A., *Good and Proper Materials: the fabric of London since the Great Fire*, London, RCHME and the London Topographical Society, 1989

—— *Regent's Park from 1086 to the present day*, 2nd edn, London, Bedford College, 1981

—— *The Regent's Park Villas*, London, Bedford College, 1981

—— (ed.) *The Royal Exchange*, London, London Topographical Society Publication No. 152, 1997

Scherren, H., *The Zoological Society of London*, London, 1905

Sennett, R., *The Fall of Public Man*, Cambridge, Cambridge University Press, 1974

Service, A., *London, 1900*, St Albans, Crosby, Lockwood, Staples, 1979

Sheppard, F., *London, 1808–1870: the infernal wen*, London, Secker and Warburg, 1971

Smith, A. R., 'Lord Elgin and his Collection', *Journal of Hellenic Studies*, II, 1916

Smith, H. C., 'Vicissitudes of Marble Arch', *Country Life*, 112, 4 July 1952, 38–9

Soane, J., *Designs for Public and Private Buildings*, London, 1828

Southey, Robert, *Letters from England, 1807*, reprinted Gloucester, Alan Sutton, 1984

Stroud, D., 'Hyde Park Corner', *Architectural Review*, 106, 1949

Summerson, J., 'The Beginnings of Regent's Park', *Architectural History*, 20, 1977, 56–62

—— *Georgian London*, Harmondsworth, Penguin, 1978

—— *John Nash Architect to King George IV*, London, Allen and Unwin, 1949

—— *The Life and Work of John Nash, Architect*, London and Cambridge, Mass., Allen and Unwin, 1980

The Survey of London, XX, Trafalgar Square and the parish of St Martin in the Fields, III, London, 1940

Taylor, F. H., *The Taste of Angels: a history of collecting from Rameses to Napoleon*, London, Hamish Hamilton, 1948

Vidler, A., *The Architectural Uncanny: essays in the modern unhomely*, Cambridge, Mass., MIT, 1992

The Villas in Regent's Park and their Residents, The Marylebone Society, London, 1959

Walker, R., *The Savile Row Story*, London, Prion, 1988

Warner, M. (ed.) *The Image of London – Views by Travellers and Emigres, 1550–1920*, London, Barbican Art Gallery, 1987

Watkin, D., *Sir John Soane and Enlightenment Thought: the Royal Academy Lectures*, Cambridge, Cambridge University Press, 1995

—— 'Soane and the Picturesque: the philosophy of association' in D. Arnold (ed.) *The Picturesque in late Georgian England*, London, The Georgian Group, 1995

—— *Thomas Hope and the Neo-classical Idea*, London, Murray, 1968

White, R. J., *From Waterloo to Peterloo*, Harmondsworth, Penguin, 1968

Wilson, E., 'The Invisible Flâneur', *New Left Review*, 191, 1992

Williams, John, *An Historical Account of Subways*, London, 1828

Wolff, J., 'The Invisible Flâneuse: women and the literature of modernity', *Feminine Sentences: essays on women, culture and modernity*, Oxford, Polity Press, 1990

Wolfreys, J., *Writing London*, London and New York, Macmillan, 1998

Yarrington, A., *The Commemoration of the Hero 1800–1864: monuments to the British victors of the Napoleonic Wars*, New York and London, Garland Publishing, 1988

Young, K., *Metropolitan London: politics and urban change*, New York, Holmes and Meier, 1982

Index